W9-AHB-893

★ The Korean War ★

LIFE AS A POW

Titles in the American War Library series include:

The Korean War
Life of an American Soldier
Strategic Battles
The War at Home
Weapons of War

The American Revolution
The Civil War
The Cold War
The Persian Gulf War
The Vietnam War
The War on Terrorism
World War II

AMERICAN
WAR LIBRARY
★ ★ ★ ★

★ The Korean War ★

LIFE AS A POW

by Michael J. Martin

LUCENT
BOOKS®

THOMSON
★
™
GALE

San Diego • Detroit • New York • San Francisco • Cleveland • New Haven, Conn. • Waterville, Maine • London • Munich

© 2004 by Lucent Books. Lucent Books is an imprint of The Gale Group, Inc.,
a division of Thomson Learning, Inc.

Lucent Books® and Thomson Learning™ are trademarks used herein under license.

For more information, contact
Lucent Books
27500 Drake Rd.
Farmington Hills, MI 48331-3535
Or you can visit our Internet site at http://www.gale.com

LIBRARY OF CONGRESS CATALOGING-IN-PUBLICATION DATA

Martin, Michael J., 1948–
  Life as a POW / by Michael J. Martin.
    p. cm. — (American war library. The Korean War)
  Includes bibliographical references and index.
  Contents: The long journey northward—The permanent camps—The war inside the
camps—Keeping hope alive—A bittersweet freedom—Legacy of an unpopular war.
    ISBN 1-59018-260-X (lib: alk. paper)
  1. Korean War, 1950–1953—Prisoners and prisons, American—Juvenile literature.
2. Prisoners of war—United States—Juvenile literature. 3. Prisoners of war—Korea
(North)—Juvenile literature. [1. Korean War, 1950–1953—Prisoners and prisons.
2. Prisoners of war.] I. Title. II. American war library: Korean War.
  DS921.M227 2004
  951.904'27—dc21
                                                                    2003010514

✮ Contents ✮

A Nation Forged by War

The United States, like many nations, was forged and defined by war. Despite Benjamin Franklin's opinion that "There never was a good war or a bad peace," the United States owes its very existence to the War of Independence, one to which Franklin wholeheartedly subscribed. The country forged by war in 1776 was tempered and made stronger by the Civil War in the 1860s.

The Texas Revolution, the Mexican-American War, and the Spanish-American War expanded the country's borders and gave it overseas possessions. These wars made the United States a world power, but this status came with a price, as the nation became a key but reluctant player in both World War I and World War II.

Each successive war further defined the country's role on the world stage. Following World War II, U.S. foreign policy redefined itself to focus on the role of defender, not only of the freedom of its own citizens, but also of the freedom of people everywhere. During the Cold War that followed World War II until the collapse of the Soviet Union, defending the world meant fighting communism. This goal, manifested in the Korean and Vietnam conflicts, proved elusive and soured the American public on its achievability. As the United States emerges as the world's sole superpower, American foreign policy has been guided less by national interest and more by protecting international human rights. But as involvement in Somalia and Kosovo proves, this goal has been equally elusive.

As a result, the country's view of itself changed. Bolstered by victories in World Wars I and II, Americans first relished the role of protector. But, as war followed war in a seemingly endless procession, Americans began to doubt their leaders, their motives, and themselves. The Vietnam War especially caused people to question the validity of sending its young people to die in places where they were not particularly wanted and for people who did not seem especially grateful.

While the most obvious changes brought about by America's wars have been geopolitical in nature, many other aspects of society have been touched. War often does not bring about change directly, but acts instead like the catalyst in a chemical reaction, accelerating changes already in progress.

Some of these changes have been societal. The role of women in the United States had been slowly changing, but World War II put thousands into the work force and into uniform. They might have gone back to being housewives after the war, but equality, once experienced, would not be forgotten.

Likewise, wars have accelerated technological change. The necessity for faster airplanes and more destructive bombs led to the development of jet planes and nuclear energy. Artificial fibers developed for parachutes in the 1940s were used in clothing of the 1950s.

Lucent Books' American War Library covers key wars in the development of the nation. Each war is covered in several volumes, to allow for more detail, context, and to provide volumes on often neglected subjects, such as the kamikazes of World War II or the weapons used in the Civil War. As with all Lucent books, notes, annotated bibliographies, and appendixes such as glossaries give students a launching point for further research. In addition, sidebars and archival photographs enhance the text. Together, each volume in the American War Library will aid students in understanding how America's wars have shaped and changed its politics, economics, and society.

Forgotten Soldiers of a Forgotten War

The Korean War lasted from June 1950 to July 1953. It was fought on the Korean Peninsula, an area of land about the size of Utah. On one side were Communist troops from North Korea and China; on the other were South Korea and forces backed by the United Nations (UN). The Communists fought to unite the countries of North Korea and South Korea under one government. Meanwhile, the UN regarded the North Korean invasion of South Korea as an example of Communist aggression that had to be stopped. The majority of UN troops sent to Korea were Americans and, in a little over three years of bloody fighting, nearly thirty-seven thousand of them died. During that same time period more than seven thousand Americans were taken prisoner by the North Koreans or the Chinese. Those who survived their captivity to return home would become the most maligned victims of any conflict in American history.

War Like No Other

The fighting that began on the Korean Peninsula in the summer of 1950 was the first major conflict of the Cold War, the four-decade-long struggle between the forces of communism and the forces of democracy. Soldiers and airmen captured by the enemy in Korea were thrust into an environment never before faced by American POWs. Not only was the level of brutality toward prisoners unprecedented (three thousand American POWs died during a period of only six months), but the POWs had to endure countless indoctrination sessions specifically designed to destroy their individuality.

Since the Communists saw the prison camp as an extension of the battlefield, they kept up a relentless physical and mental assault in order to bend prisoners' wills to their own purposes. The ultimate aim, as Dr. Charles Mayo once explained after conducting a study on the treatment and behavior of American POWs as a part of a congressional investigation, was to "disintegrate the mind of an intelligent victim, to distort his sense of values to a point where he . . . will become a seemingly willing accomplice to the complete destruction of his integrity."[1]

While POWs in Korea were locked in a struggle with an insidious enemy, the American public remained relatively uninterested and uninformed. Unlike World War II, the Korean War never had popular support. With the memory of World War II still strong, the nation had little enthusiasm for fighting another war halfway around the world in a place few people had ever heard of.

When, after three years of bloody fighting, the war ended inconclusively, there was a sense of frustration that colored the homecoming of returning POWs. The war had not ended gloriously and, in fact, was widely regarded as a loss—the first ever for America in the international arena. By the mid-1950s most Americans simply wanted to forget this war. In the process, however, they came close to forgetting the men who fought it.

An American POW sits dazed in disbelief following his release. North Korean and Chinese captors subjected UN POWs to severe physical and mental torture.

Recognition a Long Time Coming

Ironically, the success of Communist propaganda in the United States was part of the reason that returning POWs received such a lukewarm reception. Although the vast majority of POWs behaved honorably, a minority made statements and radio broadcasts for the Communists. These "confessions" were obtained after incredible physical and mental duress, including ingenious forms of torture. Widely publicized throughout the world, the anti-American statements created the impression that all or most Korean War POWs had collaborated with the enemy. That negative characterization was further emphasized after the war when numerous magazine articles, books, and movies decried the "weakness" of American POWs.

Army captain Louis Rockwerk was among those former prisoners who became bitter and cynical after returning to the United States. When a superior officer accused him and all returning Korean War POWs of collaborating with the enemy, Rockwerk lost his temper, struck the officer, and was subsequently reduced in rank. Years later he explained what upset him the most about the reception he and other POWs received:

What I resent most of all is that nobody, and I'm talking about the president of the United States [then Dwight D. Eisenhower], a former general, stood up and said, "Hey, these guys are American boys and they fought in Korea, and they fought the best they could. Yes, some of them were collaborators, but don't paint them all with that brush." Nobody said a thing. Nobody spoke in our defense.[2]

Like Rockwerk, many Korean War POWs harbored deep resentments. A strong case could be made that they suffered more than prisoners of any other American war, yet they returned home to indifference, misunderstanding, and outright suspicion. The lack of appreciation for their sacrifices only complicated their readjustment to civilian life. The physical and mental aftereffects of their brutal imprisonment haunted many Korean POWs for the rest of their lives. Meanwhile, returning POWs from Vietnam, a war that the United States indisputably lost, were welcomed home as heroes.

The Korean War has often been called the forgotten war. Few of its POWs would disagree. They paid a heavy price for being part of the first UN effort to counter aggression after World War II. That effort, despite all the claims otherwise, was ultimately successful. An invading country was prevented from taking over its neighbor. Still, not until the 1990s—particularly after the dedication of the Korean War Veterans Memorial in Washington, D.C., in 1995—did the nation begin to accord those who fought and were imprisoned in Korea the recognition they deserved.

11

Chapter 1

The Long Journey Northward

T he majority of American soldiers and airmen who became POWs during the Korean War were captured during the two massive Communist offensives that were launched during the first year of the war. The first of that group were taken prisoner in South Korea after the North Koreans invaded that country in the summer of 1950. Ill-trained and poorly equipped, they had been rushed to the front when President Harry S. Truman hastily committed troops to help South Korea defend itself against the North Korean invasion. Others were captured after three hundred thousand Chinese soldiers entered the war several months later when the fighting had moved back into North Korea. No matter where they were actually captured, most Americans did not reach permanent places of imprisonment until they had endured months of nearly unimaginable hardship.

Immediately after capture they were marched away from the front lines. Their ultimate destinations were prison camps in the northernmost areas of North Korea near the Yalu River, which forms the border between China and North Korea. Most of these permanent camps, however, were not set up to receive prisoners until the spring of 1951. Meanwhile, as POWs were shuttled from place to place in North Korea, they experienced a level of brutality unprecedented in previous wars.

Death marches, massacres, and inhumane treatment in temporary camps led to thousands of fatalities. During the first six months of captivity at least 43 percent of the soldiers and airmen under North Korean control died. By comparison, 4 percent of POWs held by the Germans and Italians in World War II died.

Overrun by the Enemy

The invasion that started the Korean War began on June 25, 1950, when approximately ninety thousand North Korean combat troops launched a surprise attack on South Korea. Their goal was to unite North and South Korea under a Communist government. Since South Korea's army had only sixty-five thousand mostly inexperienced combat troops, no air force, no tanks, and no antitank weapons, the North Koreans advanced very quickly. The UN, including the United States and fifteen other countries, quickly sent troops to aid the South Koreans. But the first American troops to arrive on the scene were far from combat-ready. While some of the older of-ficers had fought in World War II, the soldiers' average age was only twenty. Most had come from duty in Japan, a relatively easy station. Few had any battlefield experience. Quickly flown to South Korea, the bewildered troops were immediately moved to the front lines to block the fast-moving Communist advance.

The United Nations was swift in deploying troops to Korea after the Communist North Korean People's Army (NKPA) invaded South Korea in 1950.

They soon discovered that the North Korean army was well trained and better equipped than they were. The worst problem was that the Americans had almost no defense against the North Koreans' Russian-built T-34 tanks. In the beginning UN forces, of which Americans were a vast majority, had no tanks of their own and their main antitank weapon, the bazooka, proved completely useless. Even with a direct hit, the rockets just bounced off the Russian tanks. Time and again, the Americans would set up blocking positions on major roads only to see the Communists move around and behind them. Once they had an American unit isolated, the North Koreans would move in for the kill. Outnumbered and outgunned, the Americans fought until they ran out of ammunition. At that point their only option was to try to evade the enemy troops and make it back to friendly forces.

An Enemy Without Mercy

American soldiers and airmen who were unfortunate enough to be captured soon discovered that they would not be treated humanely. The experience of U.S. Army major Ambrose Nugent was typical. His unit was overrun during a North Korean attack on a hill south of Seoul, South Korea, on July 5, 1950. Alone and out of ammunition, he soon saw evidence of the kind of brutality that characterized the treatment of American POWs during the Korean War. From a hiding place he watched in horror as a group of North

Korean soldiers systematically killed thirty-three wounded U.S. soldiers with rifles and bayonets.

Not long afterward, when his hiding place was discovered, Nugent was kicked and beaten bloody by soldiers using fists, feet, and rifle butts. The beating was bad enough; but like other POWs who survived their capture, Nugent was about to discover that not just his body but his mind was going to be a target. The Communists were intensely interested in the propaganda value of getting prisoners to change their minds and admit that communism was a superior form of government. With his hands tied behind his back with wire, Nugent was marched off toward Seoul. Three days later, after a grueling twenty-four-hour interrogation concerning military matters, Nugent was told he would be making a radio broadcast to thank the North Koreans for providing him with such humane treatment.

Taken to a radio station, he was shoved into a recording booth and ordered to read a speech someone had composed for him. When he refused, he was beaten again with fists and the butt of a tommy gun. Then a guard used the end of his pistol to break all the teeth on the one side of Nugent's jaw. When he still refused to make the speech, the North Koreans began to remove his fingernails with a pair of pliers.

At that point he agreed to make the speech, in which he told listeners, "It is really most generous of the North Koreans to forgive us and give us kind consideration for our health, for food, clothing, and habitation."[3]

As Nugent's ordeal suggests, POWs experienced intense emotional shock when they realized the kind of brutality they were going to be subjected to. That shock was intensified by feelings of utter helplessness. Army corporal Donald McAllister never forgot how powerless he felt in the aftermath of a fierce battle in North Korea on December 1, 1950, not long after Chinese forces entered the war. Knocked unconscious by an exploding grenade, he awoke as he was being loaded onto a U.S. Army truck full of wounded men. The truck was attempting to leave the area when it was hit by machine gun fire and the driver was killed. As McAllister remembered,

Then the tailgate was jerked open. Chinese and North Koreans were pulling men out of the truck. The North Koreans jerked us around like we were animals. I managed to crawl out, but many of the men couldn't. After more yelling, the North Koreans started throwing gasoline into my truck and the one ahead. Three of us tried to stop it, but the Koreans knocked us down and held us. One of them set fire to the trucks. After we got up, we had to stand watch and listen to our men screaming while they burned alive. The Koreans stood there and laughed. I forgot my own pain. The

tears rolled and froze in my whiskers. That was the worst day of my life.[4]

The Prisoner Problem

Soon after, McAllister and the twenty or so other prisoners still alive overheard the North Korean and Chinese soldiers arguing about their fate. The North Koreans wanted to shoot them all; the Chinese wanted to move them north as prisoners. The Chinese prevailed, but the dispute was evidence of the lack of a firm policy regarding prisoners.

Unprepared to deal with large groups of captured soldiers and airmen during the war's first months, the Communists did not know what to do with them. The North Koreans often could see no reason for keeping prisoners under their control alive. The Chinese were more apt to see the potential propagandist value of POWs. In time, holding areas were set up far to the north. Prisoners were held there while more permanent camps were being built along the Yalu.

But reaching these temporary camps meant marching over hundreds of miles of rough terrain under the worst conditions imaginable. At gunpoint and with their hands tied behind their backs, POWs had to march at a brisk pace day after day. Many had no warm clothing; some had no shoes. Inadequate food and the lack of medical treatment for the wounded increased the suffering. Those who had trouble keeping up were shot or bayoneted. Army private first class Donald

A North Korean soldier guards some of the first American POWs of the war. Prisoners had little reason to believe they would receive humane treatment.

Barton recalled what it was like for POWs on the march. "We walked for 30 days, poked and prodded with bayonets, so tired that only fear of being bayoneted and left for the crows kept us going. Many died en route, some bayoneted, some from dysentery or other diseases. The guards were merciless."[5]

As they marched north, the POWs resigned themselves to being killed at any moment. The stories they had heard about previous North Korean atrocities were not comforting. In mid-August 1950, for example, UN troops recapturing a hill near the town of Taegu, South Korea, found the corpses of twenty-six captured Americans. The only survivor told how he and the others had been forced to haul water and ammunition, and then were herded, hands tied behind backs, into a ravine. Four Koreans then fired burp guns until all the men appeared dead.

Tunnel of No Return

Even worse atrocities occurred en route to North Korea. Sixty American prisoners, for example, were gunned down in the yard of a Taejon prison in the fall of 1950. But the most notorious massacre of POWs occurred in late October of 1950, when

UN troops reached Pyongyang, the North Korean capital. Communist forces fleeing the city jammed more than one hundred American POWs into open railcars and sent them toward the northwest. On October 30 the train entered a tunnel ten miles north of the town of Sunchon. Valder John, a U.S. Army soldier captured in July, recalled what happened next:

> The train stopped in the tunnel, and the guards ordered us off. One of them told me to get twenty-five men together because we were going to eat. They gave us these little bowls for our food and told us to line up and follow them. They put us in a small ravine and told us to sit down and wait for our food. We sat down, and they started shooting us. I was shot in the arm and fell down. The guy next to me got hit in the leg and his blood splattered all over my face and head. When they got through shooting, they came around and stepped on everybody and pounded on them with their rifle butts. If anybody moved or they thought you were alive, they shot or bayoneted you. They pounded on my back and stuck a bayonet in my side, but not very deep. I just laid there. I guess what saved me was all that blood spattered on me.[6]

John's group was one of several that suffered a similar fate outside the tunnel that day. He and twenty others survived their wounds, but at least sixty-eight American prisoners died in what came to be known as the Sunchon Tunnel Massacre. Still, it might be argued that those who died at Sunchon suffered less than those forced to continue their journey to the north.

A Halloween Death March

The worst of these treks was called the Tiger Death March. (The Tiger was the nickname POWs gave to the brutal North Korean major who led it.) It began on Halloween of 1950 when 845 prisoners were gathered in a cornfield outside Manpo, North Korea. The group included 80 non-Korean civilians—mostly religious workers, teachers, and their families who had been imprisoned when the war began. The Tiger announced that anyone who felt too sick or lame to make the march should simply step aside and lie down in the cornfield. A number of grateful, unsuspecting people took him up on his offer. After the remaining prisoners and guards moved out into the surrounding mountains, those left behind were promptly shot.

The temperatures were frigid in the mountains, yet most of the POWs wore only remnants of the summer uniforms they had been captured in. Malnourished and suffering from numerous diseases and untreated wounds, they were pushed relentlessly forward by the Tiger. No pace was fast enough. They walked by day and rested by night, often sleeping in open fields. When weakened soldiers had trouble

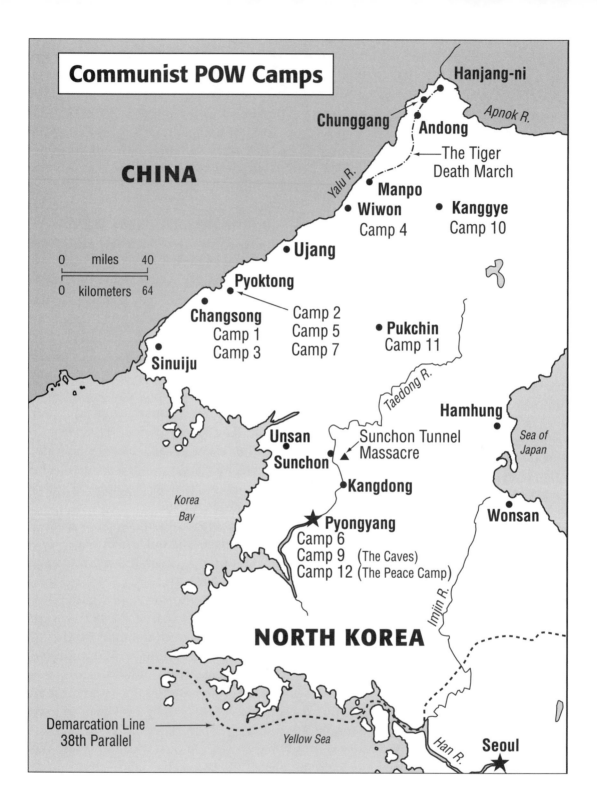

Communist POW Camps

Hanjang-ni

Apnok R.

Chunggang **Andong**

The Tiger
Death March

CHINA

Manpo
Wiwon **Kanggye**
Camp 4   Camp 10

Yalu R.

Ujang

0   miles   40

0   kilometers   64

Pyoktong

Changsong   Camp 2
Camp 1   Camp 5
Camp 3   Camp 7

Pukchin
Camp 11

Sinuiju

Taedong R.

Hamhung

*Sea of
Japan*

Unsan   Sunchon Tunnel
Massacre
Sunchon

*Korea
Bay*

Kangdong

Wonsan

★ **Pyongyang**
Camp 6
Camp 9 (The Caves)
Camp 12 (The Peace Camp)

Imjin R.

NORTH KOREA

Demarcation Line
38th Parallel

Yellow Sea

Han R.

★ **Seoul**

keeping up, the Tiger became enraged. One day he called the march to a halt and, in front of the assembled group, personally executed Lieutenant Cordus Thornton, a brave young officer who stepped forward to take the blame for his men not moving fast enough.

Larry Zellers, a teacher at an American missionary school, described the horror of Thornton's final moments as witnessed by himself and the other POWs:

> The Tiger handed a small towel to a guard. Another towel was used to tie the victim's hands behind his back. The Tiger's moves were fast and efficient. He threw off the large padded coat he was wearing, revealing his rank. . . . "You see," The Tiger said, pointing to the epaulettes on his shoulder, "I have the authority to do this." He moved smartly to face the victim and ordered him to turn around. Pausing for a moment, The Tiger pushed up the back of Thornton's fur hat. But . . . I had seen too much already; my eyes snapped shut just before The Tiger fired his pistol into the back of Thornton's head.[7]

Afterwards, the Tiger called for a translator. His message only increased the POWs' feelings of helpless outrage: "You have just witnessed the execution of a bad man. This move will help us to work together better in peace and harmony."[8]

Thornton's murder was followed by many others in the days to come. At first, the stronger prisoners helped the weaker ones keep up, but then the Tiger ordered that no prisoner could aid another. Whenever a man or woman (there were elderly nuns and teachers among the civilians) slowed their pace for any reason they were killed. The civilians were in better shape because, unlike the soldiers, they had not been malnourished and mistreated for months. Reverend Philip Crosbie, an Australian priest, recalled how awful it was to pass exhausted soldiers sitting or lying by the roadside attended by guards who waited for everyone else to pass. "Then, each time, we listened in dumb anguish for the sound that always came—the sound of a shot behind us on the road."[9]

As the other POWs heard gunshot after gunshot to their rear they struggled to come to grips with what was happening. Larry Zellers described what many of the prisoners were feeling:

> The pitiful sight of those hopeless men, younger than I, lying by the side of the road awaiting their execution took away all feelings of fatigue, hunger and cold. There were a million things to think about, but my mind refused to make a choice—perhaps because any choice would involve pain. One young man, as his last earthly act, was singing "God Bless America" as loudly as his weak cracking voice was able. Tears were streaming down his face as we marched past. There were tears on our faces as well.

I was staggered by feelings of hopeless-ness and grief.[10]

After nine grueling days and nights the Tiger Death March ended at a temporary camp at Chunggang. The march covered only one hundred miles, but the bodies of at least 100 POWs had been left behind in the snow. They were not the only casualties; twelve months later, less than 300 of the 845 who began the Tiger Death March

POWs forced along the brutal Tiger Death March hiked over one hundred miles of mountainous territory near the Chinese border.

were still alive. That was a fatality rate of about 65 percent. By comparison the Bataan Death March of World War II—probably the most infamous death march of all—had a fatality rate of 40 percent.

When the exhausted POWs finally reached the temporary camp their ordeals were not over. Winters in North Korea are notorious for their severity, but the winter of 1950–1951 was the coldest in a quarter century. And the dwellings used to house prisoners were often little more than flimsy shacks with grass roofs—or even lean-tos. Some prisoners were kept in mine pits or in caves dug into hillsides. For men weakened by disease, untreated wounds, and hunger, survival was a daunting prospect.

The Temporary Camps

At least four thousand UN prisoners (mostly Americans) went through the temporary camps during the winter of 1950–1951. The camps were places of extreme misery; for those unlucky enough to spend several months there, the death rates approached 50 percent.

POWs gave these first camps names like Mining Camp, Bean Camp, or the Valley. The temporary camp known as Death Valley held more POWs than any other. It was sixty-five miles south of the Yalu River and was first used in December 1950. Set in a deep ravine flanked by mountains, Death Valley was a place rarely reached by sunshine. A pamphlet published by the American Ex-Prisoners of War in 1981 provides this description:

Death Valley was divided into two sections, north and south, about two miles apart, and officers were placed in the south section. The north section was

Synchronized Sleepers

Raymond B. Lech, author of *Broken Soldiers*, explained how the crowded conditions at Death Valley may actually have saved some lives.

No matter how uncomfortable the crowding, the extremely cramped conditions at Death Valley saved many because they could share the only heat available—each others' bodies. The average living space, about the size of a small dining room, held thirty men. During the day, a man would sit grasping his spread knees tightly to his chest, then another man would slide backward between the first man's knees and grab his own. This would be repeated twenty-eight more times until all were tightly squeezed into the same position. At night in some rooms, sleeping was carried out in shifts, with a third standing, a third sitting, and the final third lying down.

Occupants of each room developed their own system of how to sleep. Lt. Jeff Erwin slept next to Capt. Robert Wise, and the captain woke the lieutenant about six times a night for two months so Erwin would turn him over and allow him to do the same. Another prisoner from Portsmouth, Ohio, Joel Adams, had a similar problem and remembers, "We laid on the floor and there would be so many men on each side of the room and the room was so small and crowded that we were forced to sleep on our sides; if you wanted to change from your right to your left side you had to wake up all the men in the room and change over from the right side to the left side or vice-versa."

Death Every Day

In his book, *Last Seen Alive*, author Laurence Jolidon provides testimony from U.S. Army corporal Walter R. Williams concerning the high prisoner-mortality rate during the horrible winter of 1950–1951. Williams was marched first to a camp called Death Valley, and later to Camp Five, the Communist's main camp on the Yalu River. Williams recalled that two out of every three men in the camp eventually died:

> During 1951 I was assigned to grave detail nearly every day. The greatest number of men to be buried in one day was 85 and there were never fewer than 12 a day in burial detail. Two to four men had to carry each body due to the distance from the camp to the places used for burial. Men died from the intense cold and lack of food and medical care.

approximately half the size of the south section. In the south section there were six barracks-like buildings with four to six units per barracks. A unit consisted of a room and a kitchen area. There were twenty-five men in [a] unit—so crowded that two-thirds of the group had to sit with their knees under their chins while the remaining one-third lay down. The men rotated positions. Korean-type floor heating was used, but wood was so scarce that heat was available for only one hour each day. Food consisted of 400 grams [14 ounces] of cracked corn per man per day.[11]

The number of prisoners who entered Death Valley is uncertain; estimates

range up to three thousand. But historians agree that more prisoners died there than at any other temporary camp—between five hundred and eight hundred in the few months the camp operated.

The Worst Winter

POWs who survived the war and returned home afterward recalled that the time spent in temporary camps in the winter of 1950–1951 was the low point of their captivity. The experience of First Lieutenant William H. Funchess of the U.S. Army was typical. He arrived at the Valley, a small camp, in early December. Because of a wounded foot, he was placed in a mud hut with twelve other wounded soldiers. The mood inside the dark, windowless building was almost too grim for words:

> Inside the room in the valley were the most downcast men I had ever seen. All of us had been wounded, some seriously. All of us would have quickly recovered if we had received just basic medical attention. But there was no drugs or painkillers. There were no bandages to keep open wounds covered. I kept complaining to the guards, but they always angrily muttered something in Chinese and abruptly turned away. I didn't know what they were saying, but assumed if translated it would mean something like, "The hell with you."

> The wounded men tried to be brave, but I would hear sobbing at night.

They often asked how long it would be before the U.S. Army would come to set them free. There were screams when the wounds became too painful to bear.[12]

During the two months that Funchess spent in the Valley the prisoners received no meat or vegetables of any kind. Since there was plenty of snow outside the POWs huts, their captors made no effort to provide them with water either. The only food they received was a few ounces of corn twice a day. But the corn was the kind that farmers feed to chickens. It was not enough to keep men alive in temperatures that dropped to thirty below zero. Most of the sick and wounded—perhaps as much as 90 percent—died in the temporary camps that winter.

The Struggle to Survive

POWs who survived that awful first winter needed to have a strong will to live. They realized they would have to use every resource available if they were ever going to go home. According to Captain Gene Lam—a surgeon with the Second Infantry Division when captured and sent to Death Valley—those who did survive the temporary camps scrounged for anything at all with food value. Ravenous POWs ate dogs, cats, rats, weeds, and even maggots. Simple starvation claimed many victims.

For some prisoners the lack of food was not the biggest problem. "Even worse

Some POWs ate maggots to avoid starvation. During the war's first year, POWs were rarely given any meat or vegetables to eat.

than the food was the filth we lived in," recalled Sergeant Eugene L. Inman. "It was eight months following my capture before I was permitted to remove my clothes. When I did they were alive with lice."[13]

Under such conditions diseases flourished. Death was most often caused by diarrhea, dysentery, or pneumonia. During the coldest part of the winter the frozen ground made it impossible to bury the dead. Bodies were stacked up in all the camps, but the problem was greatest in Death Valley.

In late January 1951, those prisoners who could still walk left Death Valley for Camp Five, one of five large permanent camps farther north near Pyoktong. Between 250 and 300 sick and wounded were left behind. Less than half of them survived to make the march to Camp Five some

seven weeks later. By then the other temporary camps were also being disbanded.

The last of these in operation, Bean Camp, was 35 miles south of Pyongyang. In mid-April its six hundred or so inmates left on a 160-mile trek to the northwest. When the march ended some twenty-one days later, fewer than three hundred prisoners were still alive. It was the last death march of the Korean War.

By late spring 1951 most American POWs had arrived at one of the five permanent camps set up near the south bank of the Yalu River. After months of forced marches, brutality, and starvation, the danger of imminent death seemed to be lessening. By then the Chinese had taken over the camps. Unlike the North Koreans, they seemed to have some interest in whether their prisoners lived or died.

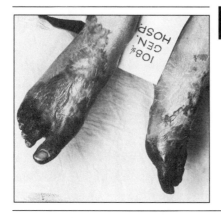

Chapter 2

The Permanent Camps

During the summer of 1951, most POWs began settling into the routines of the camps that would be their homes for the remainder of the war. Five main permanent camps, set up along the Yalu River and run by the Chinese, housed the majority of American POWs. Although the physical treatment of the prisoners in the permanent camps was better than under the North Koreans, it still failed to meet the international standards set by the Geneva Convention on Prisoners of War. Those held captive were supposed to have their condition monitored by the Red Cross to ensure they received mail and packages from home and were provided at least minimal care. Instead, inadequate shelter and clothing, contaminated water, unsanitary conditions, disease, depression, and hunger plagued POWs during the two remaining years of the war.

Four of the permanent camps were clustered near the town of Pyoktong in northwest North Korea. The Chinese believed they could control POWs better if they separated them by ranks so Camps One and Three, a little southwest of Pyoktong, were for enlisted men. Camp Five, by far the largest of the camps, eventually also held only enlisted men. It was located just west of Pyoktong on a little peninsula of land that jutted into the fast-flowing Yalu. Camp Two, a camp mostly for officers, was a few miles northeast of Camp Five. Camp Four, for sergeants only, was seventy miles to the east near the town of Wiwon.

Camp Five

Although the North Koreans ran a few permanent camps—there were three near Pyongyang—the vast majority of POWs, about three-quarters of all American prisoners, spent the last two years of the war under Chinese control at Camp Five. Almost thirty-five hundred POWs were held there when Camp Five opened. The many deaths that occurred there, however, brought the number down to about twelve hundred prisoners at any given time.

Camp Five was separated from the town of Pyoktong by a barbed-wire fence and guarded by about two hundred Chinese soldiers. Another twelve hundred soldiers were stationed in the town and could be called quickly if needed. A dozen or so guard posts were set up around the camp, but there were none on one side where the fast-flowing Yalu River was a mile wide. Even if a POW somehow managed to swim across he would only be escaping farther into Communist China.

As in the temporary camps, conditions in the permanent camps were horrific at first. When First Lieutenant William H. Funchess arrived in Camp Five from the Valley Camp he saw dismayingly familiar scenes. He was placed in a mud shack, formerly the home of a Korean family, that was like the one he had just left. For men who had been told that conditions would be better in the permanent camps, it was a huge disappointment. "The Chinese had lied to us again," recalled Funchess. "They told us they had built a POW camp but I saw nothing they had constructed except the fence."[14]

Misery in the Mud

Overcrowding and inadequate shelter continued to be an unending source of misery. The huts the prisoners lived in were roughly ten feet square. They had dirt floors with walls and roofs made of mud and straw. The men were provided no blankets and the windows of their huts—when they existed—were covered with paper that provided scant protection from the cold wind. Seventeen or more men had to sleep in an unheated hut, a nightly ordeal since it was never possible for everyone to lie down at once.

The close quarters encouraged the spread of diseases like dysentery and pneumonia. Meanwhile, lice and bedbugs proliferated in the tight quarters. U.S. Army sergeant Donald Slagle was captured in the fall of 1950 and spent most of the war at Camp Five. He had vivid memories of the filth he and other POWs were forced to endure. Lice laid eggs in the seams of the POWs' clothing. After the eggs hatched the lice would suck blood from emaciated men who had precious little to spare. "The only way we had to delouse was to pick the lice from our cloth-

American POWs were forced to endure infestations of parasites like this human head louse.

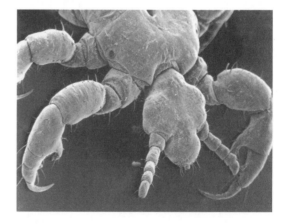

ing," Slagle remembered. "We never got them all."[15] Not until the spring of 1952 were the prisoners allowed to wash their hands, face, or hair. When the guards told the men they could bathe in the river, Slagle jumped in, clothes and all.

A Pain That Never Ended

Adding greatly to the prisoner's suffering was a hunger that never abated. Up until the last months of captivity, food dominated the thoughts of most POWs. They never seemed to receive enough. In Camp Five the usual fare was millet seed, cracked corn, and, on occasion, dried soybeans. "The pain is always there, and you think about it all day long," recalled Billy Joe Harris, an enlistee in the U.S. Army. "Food is all that sticks in your mind. When you go to sleep, you dream about it. You get up the next morning and it's the same thing."[16]

One of the reasons the men's hunger never left them was that the meager amount of food they did receive either had little nutritional value or was improperly cooked. Many prisoners would have had trouble digesting the unfamiliar diet even if it had been properly prepared. Army corporal Roy Hardage described the difficulties of eating nothing but grains for months on end and how he had to trick himself into continuing to eat:

After you eat only straight corn or barley day after day, month after month with no salt or bread to accompany it—well, this "horse feed" really gets hard to force down. But I knew damn well if I didn't eat it, I'd die. So I would try to keep my mind on something else. I would never look down at my food so I could ignore the worms in it. If you look at the same chow day after day, it will eventually crack you up. When eating it was best to get in a big argument; then, before you realized it, you had swallowed your food.[17]

Other foods consumed when available included soupy rice, cabbage, potatoes, and soybeans. The soybeans were the source of most of the protein consumed by prisoners. Protein was important because meat was rarely seen. According to army staff sergeant Thomas Gaylets, the men in Camp One got four ounces of bean milk in the morning and three ounces of rice at each of their other two meals. One memorable day they found meat in the rice. It tasted so good that the men dared to wonder whether their captors had finally decided to improve their diet. The next day they discovered the truth. A rat had gotten into the rice and the Chinese cooks had decided to make it part of the meal. "There would be no more meat," recalled Gaylets, "until 1953, when the Chinese occasionally started feeding us dog meat."[18]

A Deadly Diet

The ailments that claimed the most lives were cholera (from contaminated water), pneumonia, dysentery, pellagra, and beriberi. The foods the POWs were forced to eat simply did not provide them with enough nourishment. Army private first class Donald Elliott, a prisoner in Camp Two, recalled one stretch where the men in his company ate nothing but boiled turnips for fifty straight days. Although the food in the permanent camps was a marginal improvement over the starvation they had endured in the temporary camps, the weakened POWs continued to suffer greatly.

The poor diet aggravated all the other physical problems the men suffered from. For example, during the winter months, unable to get any kind of fresh vegetables, most POWs suffered from night blindness brought on by a vitamin deficiency. It was a strange affliction: If they looked straight ahead everything was black. But if they stared down at the ground in front of them they could see a little bit ahead out of the top portion of their field of vision. As soon as spring came, and they had eaten a few helpings of cabbage or other green vegetables, the problem vanished.

Severe malnutrition had an overall devastating effect on a soldier's health. Sergeant Eugene L. Inman recalled that the period from March 1951 to August 1952 was particularly rough for him:

> I experienced profound changes in the conditions of my body. I could not see well after dark, my sinuses bled, I would urinate blood at various times, and my kidneys hurt. Beriberi began

POWs welcomed as a treat the rat meat that was occasionally mixed in with their food.

No Place for Picky Eaters

After surviving the Tiger Death March, Wayne Simpson was determined to live until the end of the war. In Lewis H. Carlson's *Remembered Prisoners of a Forgotten War*, Simpson describes the attitude that helped him survive Camp Three:

When I first got captured I made up my mind that I was not going to give in or give up. There were some who told themselves over and over, "If I die I am out of the mess." But I was going to eat everything I could beg, borrow, or steal—clean, dirty, or otherwise. If I thought something had a little nutrition I ate it. And that just stayed with me. I think it helped that we were raised during the Depression and didn't have much to eat. We knew how to tough it out. We knew how to adjust to their changing circumstances. I can remember these guys on post before we got to Korea. They'd skip lunch and dinner and go to the snack bar. We called them "snack bar babies." Guys like me ate all three meals in the mess hall. You had to have a will to live and to eat whatever there was.

through the severe lack of vitamins, my legs would swell up, and the pain became acute. . . .

At the height of the malnutrition I had an extended abdomen, worms in my stool, sores and scales on my body, and my gums and mouth became extremely raw. That was compounded by a Chinese guard who had knocked me around for not being obedient and humble.[19]

Hospital of Horrors

The guard who roughed up Inman also succeeded in knocking out a few of his teeth. Since dental care and medical care were practically nonexistent in the camps, that kind of everyday brutality added immeasurably to the POWs' suffering. There were hospitals in the camps, but the POWs who staffed them were given almost no resources to fight a wide range of conditions. After the war, doctor and U.S. Army captain Sidney Esensten, a former POW of Camp Five, estimated that at least 75 percent of the men taken prisoner between July 1950 and September 1951 died. He added that "none of these men had illnesses that would have caused death had they been under normal conditions."[20]

The designated hospital in Camp Five was in a former Buddhist temple a distance from the rest of the camp. Captain Gene Lam, a surgeon with the Army's Second Division, was assigned there by the Chinese and told to stop the dying. But when he asked for more food and medicine he was told these could not be supplied. After his regimental surgeon died there in his arms, Lam concluded that the hospital was really just another place to die.

During the POWs' first days in the permanent camps, dysentery and pneumonia

How to Make an Entire Building Vanish

In Lewis H. Carlson's book, *Remembered Prisoners of a Forgotten War*, Captain Gene Lam, a battalion surgeon for the Ninth Infantry, relates an incident that occurred after his capture in December 1950. The Chinese let him run a makeshift hospital at Death Valley but made no provisions for heating the building during that brutally cold winter.

> They let us set up this little hospital. They gave us two fifty-five gallon drums to make a stove . . . but they didn't give us anything to burn. Right next door was one of the few buildings in Korea built with boards. Within two weeks every board and every piece of straw in it had disappeared; in fact, the whole building had disappeared. When I was called in, the commander asked me what had happened to the building. I told him, "Well, obviously you are mistaken. There is no building there." They knew we stole it, but they didn't know how.

were the big killers. Later on pellagra and beriberi, diseases brought on by extreme malnutrition, claimed the most victims. Esensten recalled how helpless he and other POWs felt as they watched men fade away. They began to see different kinds of hysteria. Some prisoners could only see what was directly in front of them. Some could not move their arms or legs, while others were completely paralyzed. "There wasn't much we could do for them," said Esensten, "unless we could catch them early in their paralysis or before coma and get some buddies to get them out and walk them day and night and force feed them until they began to eat."[21]

Many men died from what the other POWs called "give-upitis." Men simply lost the will to live. Despite the efforts of others to force them to eat, they would lie down, stare off into space, and not long after they would be dead. "It was easier to die than it was to live," recalled Lieutenant Walt Mayo. "We tried to do as much amateur psychology as we could, but the problem was sheer despair."[22]

Almost every soldier captured during the brutal winter of 1950–1951 suffered from some form of frostbite. In the camps, as prisoners lay wounded or dying, their fingers and toes would turn black. Sometimes the appendages dropped off by themselves; sometimes they had to be broken off. If the men were really unlucky, they might receive surgical treatment from the Chinese. Roy Hardage never forgot the courage of a sixteen-year-old soldier of the U.S. Army from Alabama named Tully Cox. When Cox, who had lied about his age in order to enlist, arrived at Camp One he had already lost both his feet. When gangrene set in, a Chinese with a hacksaw entered Cox's hut and began sawing away on the boy's legs. "It was about forty degrees below zero with no heat in the room, and the doctor did not use drugs or anesthetics to deaden the pain,"[23] recalled Hardage. When Cox sat up to watch the operation, even the doctor could not stand it. He pushed the teenager back down and would not let him look.

Later a Chinese woman doctor operated on Cox's legs again, fixing them so that the bones no longer stuck out. This doctor was the only Chinese person in the camp trusted by the POWs. Many men felt she genuinely wanted to help them. Unfortunately, when her concern for saving lives was noticed by the camp administrators, she was denounced and sent away. Miraculously, her rare act of compassion helped Cox survive to see the end of the war.

However, almost none of the medical care saved lives. Most of the surgical procedures were highly questionable. Lam remembered that fifty men had pieces of chicken liver soaked in penicillin inserted under their skin. This operation was supposed to prevent disease and death. Fortunately for the men who endured this experiment, part of the treatment afterward included a special diet. Their bodies eventually sloughed off the chicken livers, but the meat, eggs, and rice they received prevented them from dying of malnutrition.

Lam also witnessed mandatory inoculations that, again, the Chinese said would prevent disease. Since all the injections were given with the same dirty needle they had exactly the opposite effect: All the

A POW exhibits his gangrenous feet. Many POWs suffered from some form of frostbite during the harsh Korean winters.

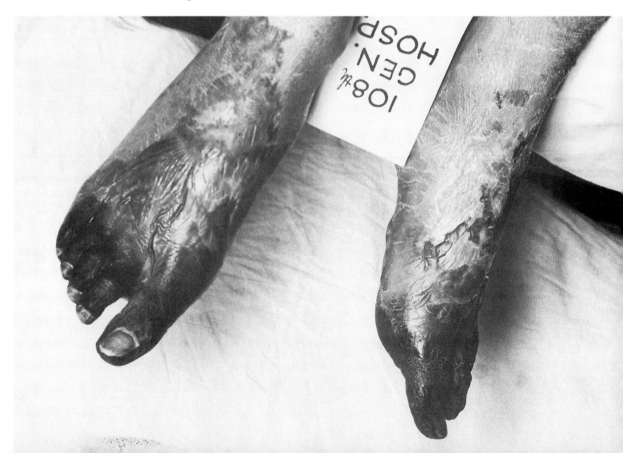

POWs who had been inoculated came down with hepatitis.

Lam and his fellow doctors tried to keep accurate records of those who died in the camps and the causes of their deaths. They figured that some day the men's families would want to know. But the Chinese did their best to ensure that any written records were destroyed. They were not eager to have the rest of the world learn that prisoners under their control were treated so poorly that they were dying of malnutrition and inadequate medical care.

Hiding Was Impossible

The treatment of POWs in the permanent camps was so brutal that prisoners inevitably entertained thoughts of escape. But that very brutality increased the difficulty of mounting an escape. By the time they had arrived at the permanent camps, most POWs had been starved and mistreated so badly that they would have had difficulty walking five miles on a level road.

And the camps where they found themselves imprisoned were hundreds of miles from the front lines. Unlike World War II, there were no neutral countries where a prisoner could count on help from sympathetic civilians. Escape to the north seemed pointless since it would mean swimming across the Yalu into Manchuria, a part of Communist China. Meanwhile, on the east, west, and south, the prison camps were hemmed in by rugged mountain ranges.

When POWs first arrived at Camp One they wondered why, unlike some of the other camps, there were no fences or barbed wire. When they questioned their captors about this, the response was, "We don't need barbed wire. Your faces are the barbed wire."[24] The Chinese were confident that the POWs' appearance contrasted so sharply with that of the North Koreans that they would soon be found if they left the camps. As marine colonel William Thrash put it, "Being a Caucasian, you'd be bound to stand out like a white horse walking down Main Street."[25] The U.S. Army's Robert Fletcher, a black soldier imprisoned at Camp Five, noted the same thing about the color of his skin. Fletcher added that, since none of the POWs were allowed to shave, their bushy beards were a dead giveaway; Koreans tend to have scraggly beards. "You could spot an American by his height and the way he walked," recalled soldier Robert Schaefer, who was held at Camp One. "By the same token, you could spot an Asian's walk from as far away as you could see him, just by the way he took his steps. An American had no chance out there."[26] Since a successful escapee would need to find food and shelter for weeks or months while working his way south, the odds of success were slim. Sooner or later someone would see him and there was little chance a North Korean civilian would take the risk of hiding or helping an escaped prisoner. As an added incentive, the Chinese sometimes paid North Koreans who turned in escaped prisoners. Thrash recalled how, when a prisoner escaped, local school kids were let out of school to join in the search. The kids would fan out through the fields and mountains. They considered it a game and would all cheer when a prisoner was found.

An escape, of course, was not a game for the POWs. Fletcher had vivid memories of what happened following one unsuccessful attempt:

> The Communist way is to punish the person who is most liked. That punishes everybody. . . . For example, this one guy tried to escape and killed a guard. The Chinese didn't bother the guy who did it; instead, they took this fellow who was liked by everybody and tied him on a tripod and threw cold water on him in thirty-five below weather. Every hour they went out and threw a bucket of water on him until he froze to death. The Chinese then pointed to the rest of us and said, "This could happen to you, and you, and you."[27]

Despite the dangers, some men could not resist trying to make their way to freedom. Harry Falck, a prisoner at Camp Five, recalled that during his early days in the camp escapes were tried two or three times a month. None that he knew of were successful. Reluctantly, all but a handful of the POWs interned in the permanent camps resigned themselves to the idea that the only way they would be going home was if they could survive until

An Irresistible Offer

General Deng, the Chinese commander of Camp Two, bragged about the impossibility of an escape. He was so sure of himself that he made the POWs of Camp Two an offer: Any prisoner who wanted to escape could sign up—the Chinese would even pack them a lunch and give them a two-hour head start. In *American POWs in Korea*, a book edited by Harry Spiller, First Lieutenant William Funchess tells what happened after he took Deng at his word and signed up:

> I forgot about my night blindness and my injured foot. I wanted to go and foolishly assumed Deng would live up to his word. He didn't. Almost immediately I was taken out of camp for interrogation. The Chinese demanded to know why I wanted to escape. They expounded on their so-called lenient policy toward POWs. They accuse me of being a warmonger and of not being sincere. The way they ranted and raved one would have thought I had committed some terrible act. All I did was take old beady-eyed Deng up on his promise. He reneged on his deal.

the war ended. When peace talks began in the summer of 1951, most figured the war would be over in a matter of weeks anyway. In the meantime they tried to adjust to a camp routine of inadequate meals and hard labor.

Camp Work

Although few POWs were fit enough to do heavy work, they were required to do many jobs around the camp. One of the most demanding chores was searching for firewood. All the huts were heated with firewood, and, as the war dragged on, POWs had to go farther and farther afield to find wood to burn. In the mornings they were marched up into the hills in search of fuel. Once they found a tree or shrub, they had to chop up the branches and then make the journey back to camp carrying big bundles of sticks.

Despite their weak physical condition, POWs had to do much of the hard work in the camps. They dug latrines and buried men who had died of illness or mistreatment. Digging graves was an unpleasant job no matter what the season, but it was a nearly impossible task during the dead of winter. During the summers, some of the POWs were allowed to garden, though the vegetables they grew were often stolen by the guards. Prisoners in camps adjacent to the Yalu were sometimes forced to unload barges of supplies.

And the Chinese did not hesitate to assign meaningless tasks as punishment or harassment. In Camp Two, a group of forty prisoners was ordered to dig a trench sixty feet long and six feet deep. As they shoveled dirt, most of the prisoners assumed they were digging their own graves. Instead, when they finished, they had to put the dirt in sacks and carry them some two or three miles before dumping them in the mountains. The next day another group of prisoners was marched up into the mountains to the same spot. There they shoveled the dirt back into sacks, hauled the sacks back to

Breakout!

The only successful escape reported from the permanent camps occurred under unique circumstances. U.S. Army private Paul Smith was with a group of five prisoners who had been marched from Camp Five to work in some farm fields. As Smith explains in the book *American POWs in Korea*, edited by Harry Spiller, there were some trucks parked on a nearby road. When the prisoners, including Smith, noticed their guards were not watching closely they made a fateful decision. They worked as close to the trucks as they could, then made a run for them. The guards spotted them and opened fire, wounding one of the prisoners. His buddies picked him up and kept running. They jumped in the truck and took off down the road driving south as fast as they could.

When the bullet-riddled truck finally ran out of gas they left it in a ditch and began walking, carrying the wounded man with them. "We walked for most of the night and the next morning we started down a hill and I saw the most beautiful sight in my life, American troops," recalled Smith. "We had made it to freedom."

camp, and filled the hole that had been made the day before.

The jobs done by those POWs who volunteered to help with food preparation were much more meaningful. Toward the end of 1951 the Chinese began allowing prisoners to cook their own food. The primitive kitchens in use were little more than sheds with big pots hanging over a fire. Still, the opportunity to prepare meals properly helped all POWs get better nutrition from their meager diet. Each kitchen had a chief cook and a crew that was supervised by a Chinese officer and two soldiers. Some prisoners did nothing but carry water for the cook to boil. Others maintained a steady supply of firewood or made sure the fires stayed hot enough for cooking.

Coping with Captivity

Even with the improvement in food preparation, the unrelieved brutality of their surroundings made it crucial that POWs not give in to despair. Maintaining faith in the future was difficult but important—those who lost hope usually did not live long. According to Michael Cornwell, an enlisted man and former Korean POW who later became a lieutenant colonel, the prisoners who survived best kept themselves busy and were able to adjust to changing circumstances. Army enlistee Robert Maclean described the simple philosophy that kept him alive in Camp One:

> "My grandfather had a saying, 'You get used to hanging if you hang long enough.' That's the philosophy I took to prison camp. You just get used to it, even the bad food. It becomes a way of life."[28]

Prisoners had to fight off boredom and despair as best they could. The men in Thrash's hut often spent evenings singing all the songs they could remember. James Thompson of the U.S. Army and his fellow prisoners got comfort from the religious hymns they had learned as kids. At one time or another every POW became depressed or downhearted. When that happened, a man's friends would talk and laugh and try to cheer him up.

During the times they were not working or being indoctrinated, POWs shared stories, jokes, and conversation. Some played card games with cards they made out of cardboard. Chess was another pleasant and time-consuming way to keep one's mind busy. Later on, the Chinese allowed POWs to play an occasional baseball or basketball game. There were libraries in some of the camps, but the books were mostly Communist literature. Still, there were novels by authors such as Charles Dickens, Pearl Buck, and Upton Sinclair. For avid readers like Cornwell such books providing a mental escape from their depressing surroundings.

The one thing that could raise POWs' morale the most was mail from home. Yet, for the first year of the war the Communists did not allow prisoners to write or receive letters. Toward the end of 1951 they began allowing both incoming and outgoing mail, though the letters were heavily censored. The reason for their change of heart was not humanitarian. By then they had realized that mail, just like food and harsh treatment, could be used to reward or punish prisoner behavior.

POWs who had survived both the temporary camps and the permanent camps were hardened by their experience. Yet, few were prepared for the mental ordeal they would face in the remaining years of captivity.

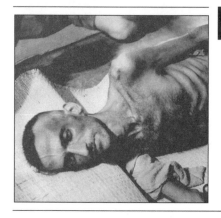
The War Inside the Camps

While physical conditions for most POWs had begun to ease somewhat toward the end of 1951, the psychological pressures actually increased. A systematic program of interrogation, indoctrination, and random brutality was used to turn the soldiers and airmen against America. How prisoners responded to the process that the Communists called "reeducation" determined the kind of treatment they would receive from their captors. Those who did not display the proper appreciation for the benefits of communism were punished severely and sometimes fatally.

Unfortunately for Americans who became prisoners during the Korean conflict, there were no recognized standards for the treatment of war prisoners. Neither North Korea nor China had signed the recent international agreement regarding POWs. Drawn up in Switzerland in 1949, the Geneva Convention set down rules for the conduct of prisoners and captors and allowed for the inspection of prison camps by neutral parties. Had neutral inspectors been allowed into North Korea, there is little doubt they would have condemned what was taking place there.

The attitudes and behavior of both the North Korean and the Chinese captors were driven by their fervent belief in communism. Since communism was seen as a perfect system, anyone who fought against it was, by definition, a war criminal. And war criminals were not entitled to humane treatment or protection. While the North Koreans used POWs as forced labor, interrogated them about military matters, and subjected them to crude forms of political indoctrination, the Chinese attitude was slightly more sophisticated.

The Lenient Policy

Chinese Communists based their treatment of Korean War prisoners on a policy developed during the revolution that brought them to power in China in 1949.

The so-called Lenient Policy had converted thousands of Chinese to communism in what one historian called "one of the most massive assaults in history on the collective mind of a people."[29] Under virtually the same policy, all Korean War prisoners were required to become friends with their captors. They were offered political education as a means of redeeming themselves and proving themselves worthy of communism. However, those who showed a lack of responsiveness or actively resisted the Communist message were subject to immediate punishment, including many sophisticated means of torture.

While the Lenient Policy supposedly showed compassion for the enemy, there was little mercy shown for those who did not embrace it. As the Chinese put it, "The Lenient Policy has its limitations as regards our enemies."[30] An official named Wong worded it much more bluntly in a talk he gave to POWs at Camp Five in April 1951:

> You are the aggressors and if you don't accept the lenient policy and change

Diplomats gather to sign the Geneva Convention in 1949. The Geneva Convention set rules for the conduct of captors and their prisoners during wartime.

your views, we have dug a hole which we are going to throw you in. . . . A person who does not accept our doctrine is not a human being because he is not for the masses and a man that is not for the masses does not deserve treatment any better than you give an animal. As an animal, we have a right to eliminate you.[31]

There was little doubt among the POWs that Wong meant what he said. As many POWs reported later, the Chinese were surprisingly friendly in the beginning. They would agree that camp conditions were bad, then suggest that prisoners and captors work together to make them better. POWs soon learned that what the Communists meant by "working together" was that they would help prisoners correct the "errors" in their thinking. Once prisoners agreed with everything their captors told them about the values of communism and renounced America's system of government, they might expect better treatment. For those who resisted, severe punishment awaited.

A Plan for Prisoners

The Lenient Policy was just a part of a well thought out plan of indoctrination. The first step was to break down American POWs' natural resistance to Communist ideology. This was accomplished by keeping prisoners cold, hungry, and disorganized. Surrounded by misery, it was hoped that they would eventually realize that their only hope for better conditions was to embrace the Communist message. A doctor at Camp Five recalled the state of mind the Communists were trying to create:

> "They waited until we could see many of our own people die . . . Until a man would say, 'Why should I die like the others? I need only listen, nod my head and say yes, and then I may get more to eat.'"[32]

From the beginning, interrogations were used to confuse and terrorize POWs. That, too, was part of the plan. Both the Chinese and the North Koreans knew that most POWs had little information of military value, but they used the interrogation process to break the men down and remind them that their lives depended on the good will of their captors. One method to increase the psychological pressure was to keep prisoners from establishing a predictable routine. A POW might be called for an interrogation, then left waiting for hours in an adjoining room. Another favorite tactic was to call a man in for questioning several times in the middle of the night.

Corporal Glenn Reynolds was singled out at Camp Five because the Chinese mistakenly thought he was an officer. He was beaten frequently when he maintained, truthfully, that he was only a corporal. Questioned for days at a time without food or water, he was periodically allowed back to his hut. As soon as he fell

"You Couldn't Clam Up"

In his book, *The Captives of Korea*, author William Lindsay White asked a former POW, identified only as "The Doctor," about ways the Communists forced prisoners to take part in their indoctrination sessions. "The Doctor" replied,

> The substance was "You have no democracy. Your country is run by the big money for its own benefit. But you soldiers are our friends. You were duped. They sent you out here to fight Wall Street's War."

> Their study materials were the New York and London editions of the "Daily Worker," plus the works of Stalin and Mao Tse-tung. "We don't expect you to agree with us at first," they explained. "We only want you to listen with an open mind. We encourage you to say anything you want to. Argue as much as you like. No man will ever be punished for disagreeing."

> We would put up heavy arguments, but [they would respond] "Comrade you haven't understood," and then would follow hours of boring repetitive argument. When they first got you to talk, they didn't care what you said. They would hammer away until you gave up out of boredom. But—and this was important—you couldn't clam up. That showed a hostile attitude! You could be punished.

into a deep sleep, he would be shaken awake and taken back for more questioning and beatings. Although Reynolds lost all track of time, fellow prisoners later told him that this went on for five days. By the end of his ordeal, he recalled, "I didn't know where or who I was or what it was I was supposed to tell the truth about."[33] That, too, was by design. Exhausted men in such a state could sometimes be persuaded to do whatever their captors wanted them to do.

Another method of breaking down POWs' resistance to Communist ideology was to tear down traditional military discipline and group solidarity. Officers and enlisted men were separated from each other and placed in different camps. African American soldiers were separated from other Americans. Natural leaders, if they could be identified, were also re-

moved from the group. The idea was to promote an every-man-for-himself attitude that would make it easier for the Communists to appeal to an individual's instinct for survival.

Studying Communism

The second step in the indoctrination of POWs involved an intensive program of formal study of communism. Lectures, reading, and writing went on for months. For about a year, prisoners spent up to ten hours a day in some form of supervised study. According to First Lieutenant William Funchess, the lectures in Camp Five began early in the morning and lasted until noon. At that time the Chinese took a half-hour break to eat lunch before the afternoon session (prisoners only received food in the mornings and evenings, so they waited while the guards content into English, a process that prisoners found excruciatingly boring.

Lectures were usually followed by smaller classes. The Communists assigned homework; POWs were furnished with papers and notebooks in which they were required to write down what they had learned after a particular lecture or reading. Some of the books the prisoners were forced to read were *The Twilight of Capitalism, The Life of Karl Marx*, and *The Decline and Fall of America*. These books were read aloud. The reader was usually a prisoner chosen by the Chinese.

Not only were POWs required to attend these classes, they had to demonstrate progress in their understanding of Marxism-Leninism and learn to admire the achievements of leaders like Joseph Stalin and Mao Tse-tung. Those prisoners who learned the fastest were called progressives and were rewarded with extra food and more frequent mail from home.

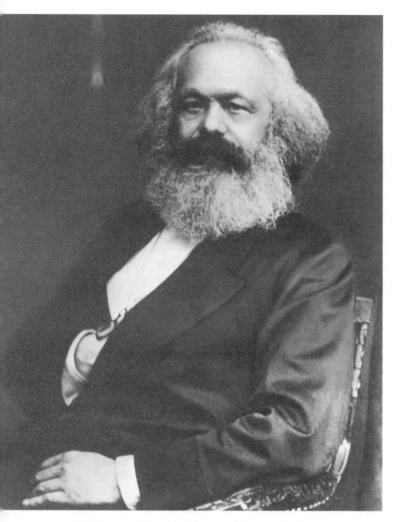

POWs were often forced to read the works of Karl Marx, a founder of communism.

ate their lunch). The indoctrination program had lessons with titles like "The Large Ruling Rich Families in the United States" and "The Decline of Capitalism." The lectures were given first in Chinese and then an interpreter translated the

A Diabolical System

The Chinese even came up with a way for the POWs to indoctrinate themselves. Since there were not enough English-speaking Communists to supervise each squad of men, the Chinese appointed squad monitors from among the prison-

Harassment with a Purpose

Journalist Eugene Kinkead, author of *In Every War but One*, relied on a U.S. Army study of POWs done after the war for many of the conclusions in his book. Here, he describes how the Communists intentionally introduced an element of uncertainty into POWs' lives:

The technique of harassment was equally successful. It was used on all the men; even the most fawning progressives were subjected to it when their captors wished greater cooperation from them. The most minor offense, deliberate or not, could set the technique in motion. Suppose a prisoner failed to answer a question in class. He was ordered to camp headquarters and given a long lecture on the grave necessity of paying strict attention to the instructor and remembering what was said. This was only the beginning. That same prisoner would be called to headquarters again, perhaps at midnight, and lectured in the same way. The next day, he might be in the latrine when he was summoned, in haste, and given another lecture on his grievous shortcomings. Then he would be aroused at two o'clock the next morning, and once again his offenses would be discussed. The Chinese knew that this treatment deprived the prisoners of what they wanted above everything else—to be left alone to lead a normal prisoner's life. The army study showed that most prisoners felt if they complied with the enemy at the time, they would be left alone thereafter. But they learned, to their sorrow, that this never happened. Harassment continued, and even increased.

ers to carry out the reading and study portion of the indoctrination program. Under this ingenious and diabolical system, approximately a hundred POWs were forced to conduct classes in communism for their fellow prisoners each day. The appointees had no choice in the matter and most intensely disliked the difficult position it put them in.

Army lieutenant Jeff Erwin was recovering from pneumonia when he refused to become a monitor. The Chinese would not accept his refusal. They forced him to stand at attention for hours while he "reconsidered" his position. The second he relaxed, a guard stationed nearby would kick him or beat him with a rifle butt. Realizing he was facing certain death if he did not change his mind, Erwin reluctantly agreed to become a monitor. Each morning he and the other unfortunate POWs who had been chosen as monitors were required to pick up a newspaper article, book, or sheet of paper with the day's topic written on it. Later they had to conduct study groups on the material for approximately six hours. After discussions about the material the prisoners were quizzed about their understanding. At the end of the day, written reports, composed either by the entire squad or by each of its members, were required to be turned in.

Their captors probably never expected to convert the majority of POWs into ardent Communists. Their real aim was to sow dissension among the troops and break down morale so that they could use some POWs for their own propaganda purposes. That was one reason that repetition was such a key element of their indoctrination. Day after day and month after month the POWs were required to study the benefits of communism.

The Dangers of Defiance

POWs who did not "learn" properly soon found out what was in store for them. Even if the lessons contradicted what they had seen with their own eyes, prisoners learned not to dispute their instructors. According to Colonel Perry, during an indoctrination one day a POW noted that if, as they were being told, the South Koreans had started the war, it seemed odd that the North Koreans had already reached the outskirts of Seoul after only one day of fighting. His comment infuriated the instructor. "You are a stupid, ignorant fool," he said. "Everyone else in the class knows the South Koreans started the war. Why don't you?"[34]

When the POW continued to demand an answer, the instructor made the rest of the class stand at attention. After several hours the man withdrew his objection. The next day the prisoner was forced to read to the class a self-criticism of his conduct and an apology. He was required to do so for the next five days, each time elaborating on his "crime." Then his classmates were ordered to criticize him. Techniques like this were designed to break down the solidarity within a group.

Still, most POWs felt they had little choice if they wanted to survive. They had seen thousands of their comrades die in the winter of 1950–1951 and they could never be certain that a wrong answer might not mean their own death. Speaking about the early days of indoctrination, one officer said, "I don't think an American is alive who defied them. I know some who defied them and are dead."[35]

In truth, a few POWs did defy the system and live. Navy helicopter pilot and lieutenant John Thornton refused to be a good student. "I did not write. I would not answer the questions," he recalled. "I would hand in a blank paper. I would say I'm not a diplomat and I don't know these things."[36]

Although Thornton's defiance did not cost him his life, others were not so lucky. Part of the strategy of the Communists was to keep prisoners off balance as much as possible, ensuring that no one knew for sure when or why they would be severely punished. After dark, the Chinese would come into the prisoners' huts with flashlights, shine them in prisoners' faces and ask questions about the day's instruction. Those who refused to answer or gave inadequate answers were beaten or punished severely. Challenging an instructor or ignoring their lessons could be fatal. One day, after a long, dull session about the writings of a prominent Communist leader, a POW named Major Thomas Hume was asked what he thought of the writing. When he told the Chinese he did not think it was worth the paper it was printed on, he was thrown in a hole without warm clothing or blankets. Hume's death after days of suffering was meant to serve as an example to the other prisoners. "It certainly had a big effect on me," recalled Funchess. "It proved to us that the Communists, indeed, were most serious in the conduct of their indoctrination."[37]

Fear, fatigue, hunger, and harassment were all used to break down a prisoner's resistance to communism. Army corporal Daniel Johnson recalled a frigid night when, although the temperature was well below zero, the men in Camp One were forced to assemble outside in the snow to watch a Russian propaganda film. While their feet and hands turned numb they watched the film, then listened to a speech about the greatness of the Communist system and the unfairness of American capitalism.

Converts to Communism?

All this forced reeducation rarely changed a POW's mind. As Sergeant First Class Harley Coon, who would one day become president of the Korean Ex-Prisoners of War Association, put it, "You can't take a person who is starving and torture him and take away everything he has been accustomed to in life, and then tell him how much better off he would be with Communism."[38]

Sergeant Walter Adelman, who spent almost two years at Camp One, summarized the effect that indoctrination had on him and most of his fellow prisoners:

They kept going over and over the Communist doctrine. They tried to cause us not to trust one another, and for a few that worked, but they didn't make any headway there either. After a while they gave us pamphlets and books to read, but that didn't work either. We just listened to them and then concentrated on surviving the war.[39]

A former POW awaits the verdict of a U.S. court-martial board. He was accused of collaborating with his Communist captors.

A Killer of Innocent People?

In his book, *Witness to War: Korea*, Colonel Rod Paschall reprints an article that appeared in a prison camp newspaper in 1951. He suggests that the POW who wrote it must have done so under pressure because he spent much of the rest of the war in solitary confinement for being a reactionary.

> Since I was liberated, I've been given time to just think and analyze this Korean problem. Often I've asked myself, "Were we paid killers?" "Are these Korean people really our enemy?" "Why am I here?" These questions have brought me to the conclusion that the American capitalists have made us nothing short of paid killers. But we were ignorant of the fact and we followed the capitalists without asking ourselves, "Why?" I am sure none of us would kill a fellow American in cold blood. But we have killed these innocent people just because MacArthur and Truman said, "they are our enemy." In reality they are a peace loving people and it is only the capitalist's lust for more power and money that had caused bloodshed. And we were the cannon fodder for their willful desires. But now we are enlightened to these facts. I believe none of us will be fooled again.

Only a tiny percentage of POWs came to truly believe that communism was a superior form of government. These men, along with those who parroted what they had been taught in hopes of better treatment, were called "progessives" by the Chinese and North Koreans. They received extra food and other favors in return for their cooperation but were usually regarded with distaste by other prisoners.

Another small percentage of POWs resisted indoctrination at every turn. Lloyd Pate of the U.S. Army was only sixteen when he was captured on January 1, 1951. He spent half of his thirty-one months as a POW in solitary confinement because he could not stand listening to lectures about how bad America was. The Communists used the term "reactionary" for men like Pate, and they either killed reactionaries outright or separated them from the rest of the prisoners.

But the vast majority of POWs in Korea did what POWs in every war have done: They kept a low profile in hopes of surviving until the war ended. Although they did not openly resist their captors, they did as little as possible to help them. In Korea, more than any other war, that was a difficult balancing act. The study system set up by the Communists, with its indoctrination classes taught by other POWs, certainly made it appear from the outside that many prisoners had gone over to the enemy side.

No Brains Were Washed

In essence, the Chinese had come up with a way to force American soldiers to teach other soldiers anti-American propaganda. After the war this led to charges in the United States that POWs must have been brainwashed to behave in such a fashion. The truth was otherwise. What occurred in Korea did not meet the definition of brainwashing. As generally understood, brainwashing means erasing an individual's personality and replacing it with a new one. There were no documented cases of that happening in Korea.

Instead, the Communists got prisoners to do what they wanted by the crude but effective technique of progressively weakening an individual's physical and moral strength through the liberal use of starvation and unrelenting brutality.

POW Michael Cornwell, an enlisted man in the army who rose to the rank of lieutenant colonel after the war, certainly did not believe he had been brainwashed:

> Some people liked to call it brainwashing. Well, it wasn't brainwashing. . . . Rather, they took the other approach: "We're going to show you what's the matter with your system.". . . It wasn't brainwashing. It was just that they wanted to tell us what was so great about themselves and what was

American POWs return from an indoctrination session. The North Koreans and Chinese tried to coerce POWs into embracing communism.

so bad about us. There was nothing subtle about it.[40]

Parading for "Peace"

The Communists eventually demanded more from POWs than just being good students. Prisoners were asked to "voluntarily" write articles about what they had learned. Stories that praised communism and criticized capitalism were put on bulletin boards or published in newspapers like Camp Five's *Truth or Peace*. The authors of the articles were rewarded with extra food or even cigarettes, a rare treat.

Next, the Chinese "suggested" that it would be a good idea if everyone in Camp Five signed a piece of paper stating that the United States was the aggressor in Korea and requesting an end to the fighting. This "Peace Appeal" was to be sent on to the UN. After a painful debate that lasted for days, the POWs in Camp Five grudgingly signed the document. Those who held out the longest against signing finally gave in after the Chinese assured them that if they did not sign, they would be sentenced to at least twenty-five years in prison and would never see their families again.

The Communists were delighted with this propaganda victory. They organized a parade to a nearby school yard and took motion pictures and still photographs. As a band played, speeches were given welcoming the POWs into the ranks of those who wanted peace in Korea. Then, everyone marched back to the camp and signed the petition. Few of the men felt good about

what they had just done. As Army major Harold Kaschko stated, "I mean, let's be honest . . . I signed the thing because I was scared of the Chinese and that's the reason the rest of them signed it."[41]

Kaschko and his fellow POWs hoped that people back in the United States would be able to tell that they were acting under great duress. But they also knew that there were some positive aspects to signing such a petition. At the time prisoners had not been allowed to send mail. By signing a petition that was sure to be released to the public, many POWs felt they would let their families back home know that they were alive. It could even be seen as a kind of insurance policy. If a prisoner appeared in a newsreel or his name appeared on a petition, the Chinese could no longer deny that he was being held captive. Up until then they could kill anyone they wanted and no one would know the difference. Once they admitted holding a prisoner, they would eventually have to answer for his treatment—if only to world opinion.

A Camp for Propaganda

World opinion was the target of several phony peace initiatives made by the North Koreans and the Chinese in 1951. From the Communist standpoint the most successful of these was organized by the North Koreans. They took a group of twenty men from Camp Five to a camp set up in Pyongyang strictly for propaganda. The number of men in Camp Twelve (the

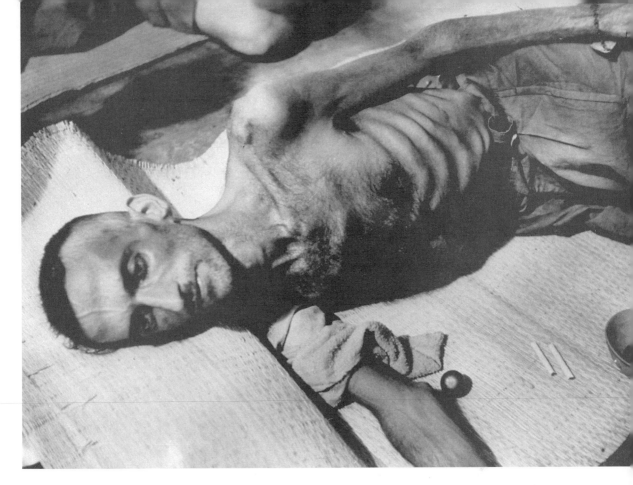

An emaciated POW lies on a mat after his release. Starving POWs was a common form of torture in Communist camps.

Koreans called it Peace Camp) eventually rose to seventy-nine. Because of the camp's small numbers and its solely propagandistic purpose, those men experienced some of the worst psychological and physical pressures of any POWs. Captain Clifford Allen recalled Camp Twelve:

They used the wild animal treatment on us. You know, when you want to tame a wild animal you starve him out first, then give him a little morsel of food. And the plan is that when you give it that little morsel of food, it loses some of its wildness and becomes a little more tame and . . . it begins to dance a little to your tune. That is the same technique they were using with us.[42]

As part of the system of control at Camp Twelve, the North Koreans kept Allen and his fellow POWs on the edge of starvation. Their sole daily rations were two small cups of millet seed. Starvation was necessary because the prisoners were asked to do things they considered abhorrent. They were there to make radio broadcasts praising communism and condemning the United States. In the first eighteen months of the war at least 215 radio broadcasts were made by POWs from Camp Twelve and other camps.

These broadcasts horrified Americans back in the United States. They doubted that American soldiers could be voluntarily making such broadcasts. It was hard to imagine what kinds of pressures could force them to make statements criticizing their own government. The pressure was indeed intense. Prisoners at Camp Twelve lived in constant fear. Besides the fear of having their meager rations cut off, they were often threatened with being sent to a place called The Caves.

The Caves

With good reason, The Caves had the worst reputation of any camp in North Korea. The life span of anyone sent there was measured in months. The camp consisted of nine caves between seventy-five and one hundred feet in length dug into a hillside. Prisoners at The Caves suffered the worst level of degradation imaginable. There were no sanitary facilities at all and their food was simply thrown at them.

The POWs at Camp Twelve were familiar with The Caves because they had to pass by them on their way to the distribution center that provided their food. Allen saw at least three hundred graves outside The Caves and also witnessed the horrific condition of its inmates. "They were skeletons —living skeletons or walking corpses, with

A Daring Plan

As reported in Raymond B. Lech's book, *Broken Soldiers*, senior officers at Camp Twelve in Pyongyang developed a plan for a daring mass escape that would have undoubtedly created worldwide headlines. An armed escape from a so-called peace camp would have had a devastating effect on the Communist propaganda of the previous two years. After the war, military experts who looked at the plan agreed that it would probably have worked.

It called for strafing of the camp by fighter planes from the U.S. Air Force, followed by the arrival of helicopters to evacuate all the prisoners in the chaos that would follow. Unfortunately, the Communists reneged on a promise that was a key element of the plan. They had promised to release two POWs as a gesture of "goodwill." Unknown to them, one of those prisoners would have had a tiny map of the camp and the escape plan sewn into a slit in his belt. When the release was canceled, the POWs lost the opportunity to let friendly forces know how to rescue them. Instead, the propaganda broadcasts continued for several more months before Camp Twelve was disbanded and its inmates sent back to Camp Five.

their eyes bulging just like bullfrogs," he recalled. "They would look at you and they didn't know who you were. . . ."[43]

At least eight prisoners from Camp Twelve were eventually sent to The Caves. Despite intense pressure to cooperate with the Communists, a minirevolt occurred in Camp Twelve on the day when the men were told they would be making a radio appeal asking American troops to lay down their arms and surrender. Despite threats that they would all be shot, the POWs stood firm and the surrender broadcast was never made.

Messages Meant for Others

In truth, few Americans actually heard any of the propaganda broadcasts made by prisoners in Korea. And if they had, not many would have been naïve enough to think American POWs were making such broadcasts voluntarily. From the Communist point of view that was not a problem—the radio shows were never intended for American audiences. Instead they were directed at developing non-Communist nations in Asia. Communist leaders in Russia and China planned to expand their ideology to other parts of the world. They believed that forcing Americans to denounce their country would help convince smaller nations that communism was the wave of the future.

The zeal to promote communism was behind much of the brutality and mental coercion experienced by POWs. Fortunately, by the end of 1951 events taking place in a town called Panmunjom in North Korea would make it possible for more and more prisoners to fight back without forfeiting their lives.

Chapter 4

Keeping Hope Alive

POWs' expectations that they would be going home soon increased in the summer of 1951 when talks to end the fighting in the Korean War began in Panmunjom. Fortunately, the truce talks led to better treatment inside the camps. As conditions improved, more and more prisoners began to feel they had a real hope of returning home alive. And the better diet they received gave many the strength to find new ways to resist indoctrination. When those negotiations stalled however, the POWs were greatly disappointed. What the POWs did not realize was that they were being held as pawns in a prolonged Cold War propaganda battle.

Not long after truce talks began, the Chinese stopped starving men to death. By then, three thousand of the seven thousand prisoners held in the camps had already died. If POWs had continued to die at the same rate, there would hardly have been any prisoners left to ex-change when the war ended. Since that might cast some doubt on the allure of communism, the Chinese and North Koreans began taking a little better care of their prisoners.

In addition, the Communists had to keep POWs alive because of a boast they had often made. They captured claimed to have as many as sixty thousand UN troops. Someone must have realized that a discrepancy between the boasted and actual numbers might cause the world to doubt that the prisoners had received adequate treatment.

A Change of Atmosphere

Still, conditions did not improve measurably until December 1951 when, as part of the truce negotiations, the Communists released the names of all their prisoners. Since the rest of the world now knew who was actually being held in North Korean prison camps, the Communists did not feel quite so free to do as they pleased inside them. The prisoners experienced an immediate change. As Sergeant Joe Gardiner put it, "Everybody was reasonably sure that the Chinese weren't going to take anyone out and shoot them because they were going to have to account for prisoners at that time; before that time they didn't have to."[44]

Throughout the remainder of 1952 and 1953, brutality still occurred but never to the degree of the war's first year. The Communists actually became a bit more lenient. Prisoners were given a little more free time and the pressures of indoctrination eased for many. Meanwhile POWs, some who had lost as much as a hundred pounds during their captivity, began to get some of the nutrition their bodies so desperately needed. Pork, fish, onions, flour, garlic, and eggs began making occasional appearances in their diet. The meat and fish often had maggots, but they were eaten anyway. Although men did not get fat on their new diet, they did lose the skeletal look of men about to die from starvation. The

UN delegates leave their tents to attend peace talks at Panmunjom. The truce talks led to better treatment of UN POWs.

strength they regained helped them to better resist Communist indoctrination.

Resisting in Secret

Resisting their captors helped POWs keep their morale up. Although there were numerous methods of resistance, the most common forms were covert. Robert Blewitt, who was imprisoned in Camp One and Camp Three, got through boring lectures by daydreaming about the beach in Atlantic City and the girls he had seen there. In Camp Five Charley Davis developed a similar method to make his indoctrination classes a little more tolerable:

> When they would start one of their propaganda sessions, I developed the ability just to turn off my mind. It took a while to be able to do this. You couldn't horse around and not appear to pay attention during these lectures because they'd rap you one. So I worked on my response, and eventually I could just stare them right in the eye and not hear a thing they said. I would just think about something else.[45]

Another covert method of resistance was compiling lists of those who died in the camps or on the way to them. Since the North Koreans and Chinese were not eager for that information to reach the outside world, putting together such a list might well prove fatal for the list maker. Still, some POWs were willing to take the risk. First Lieutenant William Funchess, for example, wrote down the names of nearly a hundred prisoners who died at Camp Two. He kept the list rolled up inside a fountain pen and eventually smuggled it back to the United States.

Army private first class Wayne Johnson, a veteran of the Tiger Death March, also risked execution by keeping track of the dead. He figured that before the names were forgotten someone should keep a record for the prisoners' loved ones. As the list grew longer, so did the danger of its discovery. "Once I started I thought there was no sense stopping," recalls Johnson. "I just thought it was the right thing to do."[46]

There were three hundred names of men who died in the temporary camps on Johnson's list when he was moved to a permanent camp. He would add another two hundred before the war ended. In October 1951, Johnson was transferred to Chinese control at Camp Three. Soon after he began compiling a master list on a piece of paper stolen from a guard's notepad.

Printing the names as small as possible, it took him several months working from the light of a crude oil lamp to complete the master list of almost five hundred names. After all that work, Johnson worried about what would happen if it were discovered and destroyed. He decided to make a duplicate list. When the backup list was finally complete, he buried one list in the floor of his mud shack and hid the other in the wall. Then, upon returning from a mandatory propaganda session one day, Johnson discovered a big hole in the wall where his list had been. Guards searching the shack had found one of his lists.

It was not long before Johnson was called in to meet with an angry camp commandant. He was ordered to sit in a chair while questions were hurled at him. "You keep this criminal propaganda list for your government!"[47] the Chinese major charged. Johnson insisted that it was not propaganda, that it was only for the families. Then the major began beating Johnson's face with a leather riding crop, demanding that he reveal who had helped him.

When Johnson insisted that no one had helped him the major grew even angrier. After a couple of hours he took out his pistol and struck the helpless POW in the head several times with the butt. Then he put the pistol to Johnson's head and cocked the hammer. "Well, fear didn't even begin to do justice to my feelings," recalls Johnson of that terrifying moment. "It was more than fear I can tell you."[48] He thought his life had come to an end, but, for some inexplicable reason, the major did not pull the trigger.

Later, when Johnson returned to his shack, he considered destroying the second list. If it were found, he would undoubtedly be executed. But then he thought of how his best friend had died of beriberi at one of the temporary camps

and was buried in an unmarked grave with no dog tags. Johnson felt an obligation to the man's family and the families of other fallen soldiers. His list remained hidden.

Guard Games

Taunting and confusing the guards was another way that POWs kept up their morale. The behavior of any group of prisoners tends to be childish because they have been placed in the position of children unable to make their own decisions. Many of the POWs' acts of defiance fit that pattern. For example, in one camp a group of prisoners spent the morning digging a hole in the middle of their compound. Then, with great ceremony they placed a piece of paper in the hole and covered it back up. Unable to resist, curious Chinese guards excavated the hole and retrieved the paper. On it were the words "Mind Your Own Business."[49]

Harry Falck recalled morning roll calls at Camp Five when all the men turned out barking like dogs. At Camp Three, navy captain and POW Henry Osborne recalled how a U.S. Navy captain named John Thornton was always playing tricks on the guards. These included riding an imaginary motorcycle around the camp. POWs at another camp would sometimes spend an hour pretending to fly around like helicopters. As Osborne put it, "Every opportunity we had we confused our captors. We held 'crazy weeks' and pulled pranks on the Chinese."[50]

"The Chicken Cannot Play with You"

Despite the grim circumstances of their captivity, POWs still occasionally found humor in their situation. One of the funniest moments —although it was not funny at the time—occurred when Robert Blewitt got caught redhanded stealing food. Blewitt had already spent a lot of time in solitary confinement for similar reactionary activities. Still, as he explains in Lewis H. Carlson's *Remembered Prisoners of a Forgotten War*, his spirit was never broken:

> Of course, I had to do all the dirty work because if any of us were going to get caught, it was going to be me. I didn't like getting caught, I just liked doing those things. I also stole chickens whenever I could. This one time I had herded them into this little building, and I'm chasing them around. They're clucking and feathers are flying. I got this one, and I'm trying to strangle him. I'm planning to smear him with mud, stuff him in our chimney, and bake him. While I'm strangling this chicken, I look out the door and sure enough here comes a Chinese guard. This chicken is just about dead, so, man, I'm trying to revive him. I'm kicking the chicken and saying, "Come on, come on, wake up, get back to life." And it did. It hopped up and started running around. The guard asked, "What are you doing with the chicken?" What was I going to say? I told him, "I'm playing with the chicken." The guard said, "The chicken cannot play with you." Off I went to the hole again.

Because most Chinese and North Koreans had a limited grasp of English and little knowledge of American ways, prisoners often amused themselves at their captors' expense. Some POWs, for example, were given questionnaires in which they were asked about their family background. Since there was no way to check the facts, the men would make up all kinds of ridiculous stories. One prisoner got away with telling the Chinese that his parents gathered moss for a living.

U.S. Air Force lieutenant Robert Carman, a prisoner at Camp Two, recalled with admiration how a fellow POW entertained prisoners while he was supposed to be reading a book about communism aloud. The feat was all the more enjoyable because it occurred right under the noses of their Chinese guards:

We'd go into this big room and sit around. This fellow named Ralph Nardello would get up to read, but while he was reading, he was also announcing a baseball game. Of course, these Chinese guys understood English, but he was able to insert this baseball game into the text. This guy was phenomenal.[51]

Open Resistance

Although it could be risky, there were numerous instances of overt resistance to Communist indoctrination. Some of the bolder POWs actually challenged their instructors. When an interpreter in Camp One told Army sergeant Douglas Tanner to speak freely, taking him at his word, Tanner asked why, if they were such a peaceful people, the Russians maintained the largest standing army in the world. For that remark, Tanner spent fifteen days in solitary confinement.

Army enlistee Robert Fletcher, an African American POW, told his captors that he did not believe them when he was told that everyone in China was equal. When he questioned whether Chairman Mao really did the same work as Chinese peasants and cooked his own food, Fletcher was called a reactionary and threatened with execution. But when he challenged his captors to go ahead and shoot him, he was labeled crazy and left alone.

Despite the danger, there were at least a half-dozen times during the war that POWs organized mass resistance to their captors. On the Communist holiday of May Day in 1952, for example, the Chinese brought the prisoners new uniforms and red banners painted with slogans. They planned to film the men marching in a parade for propaganda purposes. But the POWs passed the word that no one was to assemble for the parade. When the Chinese realized there would be no marchers they canceled the parade. Although the leaders of the boycott were punished, the rest of the men were not. On another occasion, the Chinese wanted to take propaganda pictures of a group exercising, but the prisoners refused to cooperate. When they walked away the Chinese were incensed but did nothing.

At one point the Chinese made the mistake of trying group punishment for those who most strongly resisted Communist doctrine. They set up a labor camp where 130 of the most reactionary prisoners were compelled to spend their days doing meaningless labor like hauling rocks from one place to another or digging holes and filling them up again. The plan, however, backfired badly. Instead of breaking morale, the shared hardships built stronger bonds and raised prisoners' spirits. "Everybody in that camp was a good man," recalled Dave Fortune. "Morale was much higher."[52] After a few months the Chinese realized they were building solidarity rather than tearing it down. They broke up the camp and redistributed the men back into the general POW population.

Outwitting the Censors

Eventually, most POWs were allowed to write letters home, but they soon discovered that everything they received or sent had to be approved by censors. If a letter did not contain anything about how well a prisoner was being treated, it simply did not get mailed. Meanwhile, incoming mail took months to arrive—unless it contained bad news. All correspondence from POWs' families was read first by the Chinese and then passed on when, or if, they felt like doing so. In hopes of decreasing prisoners' morale the Communists always saw that prisoners got depressing letters quickly. Most of Tanner's mail took three to six months to reach North Korea. But when his grandmother died, the news reached him in three weeks. He had barely finished reading the letter when he was called to camp headquarters and interrogated about whether the news made him sad.

Prisoners labeled reactionaries often got no mail at all. At the same time the progressives got more mail than anyone. Some POWs who refused to play the game of telling the world how wonderful their treatment was grew so disgusted with the level of censorship that they simply gave up trying to write home. Others devised ingenious methods to outwit the censors and let the world know their real situation.

Army corporal Buford McNamera, a reactionary who spent time in Camps One,

Three, Four, Five, and Nine, made the best of it when he was finally allowed to send a letter. He fooled the Chinese by writing that they were feeding him "good as his baby back home."[53] Since "Baby" was the name of the family's milk cow, everyone at home immediately understood that he was not eating well at all. A friend of POW Lieutenant Jeff Erwin conveyed a similar message about the prisoners' poor diet by writing that he was "looking forward to getting home and having dinner with Joe."[54] He realized that the Chinese had no way of knowing that Joe was the family dog. Another POW wrote about how wonderfully he was being treated and added that even his high school coach

Eating Crow

The Chinese separated African American soldiers from the rest of the prisoners in hopes of breaking down their morale. According to James Thompson, former POW and author of *True Colors*, their strategy had the opposite effect. Under the wise leadership of an older soldier whom the men in his group called Poppa Browne, they resisted indoctrination. Here Thompson recalls the humiliation of being interrogated after being punched in the mouth by his interrogator:

> I remember him walking around me a bit, surveying me suspiciously. "As for you, you disgrace to your own people. To all Third World people. You let yourself be used by a government that does not recognize you as a human being. You fool."

The old racial tactic again. They would use this many times during our captivity. Poppa

Browne had warned us over and over about the enemy's artful use of this ploy ... I can still see myself standing there boiling, my mouth cut inside and bleeding from that blow ...

"I sick of you!" the officer finally shouted, ending the session. "Get this pig outta my sight before I throw up! Get him OUTTA HERE!"

The interpreter quickly hustled me out of the room. If the outburst was meant to demean me, it was effective. I must admit to feeling quite low. I was a grown man who didn't particularly like being shouted at by anyone. But to be shouted at in a condescending manner was too much. To accept this without retaliation was even more agonizing. Captivity is no place for a proud man. There is too much crow you have to eat, especially if survival means anything.

never treated him this well. Since the coach he was referring to was a notorious hard-nosed disciplinarian, his family knew immediately that he was being treated roughly.

Rumors, Delays, and Disappointment

Tricking their captors always had a positive effect on prisoners' morale, but the rumors of imminent release that circulated through the camps tended to hurt morale badly when they did not come

true. And, unfortunately, most did not. Almost from the moment they were captured, most POWs clung to the hope that they would be going home soon because the war could not last much longer. Those hopes rose in the fall of 1950 when UN forces crossed the 38th parallel and began their march north to the Yalu River. U.S. Army general Douglas MacArthur

U.S. infantrymen march toward the 38th parallel. The hopes of POWs rose when UN forces crossed the 38th parallel in 1950.

had promised the troops they would be home by Christmas, and word of that promise reached POWs by way of newly captured prisoners. The news thrilled them and many made plans for what they would do when the war ended in a few weeks.

But the Chinese entry into the war changed all that. Some prisoners were so depressed by the realization that their suffering was going to continue indefinitely that they simply gave up, stopped eating, lapsed into a coma, and died. Dr. Sidney Esensten remembered that those who gave up were usually only eighteen or nineteen years old. "When life got to be more miserable than they could handle," he recalled, "it was easier to die than to live in misery."[55]

For those POWs who chose to live there were many more disappointments after the Chinese entry into the war. When the battle lines stabilized in 1951 and truce talks were begun that summer, it was impossible not to think that the war was entering its final stages. That fall, when a cease-fire line (a boundary that each side agreed not to advance beyond) was determined and prisoner lists exchanged, no one could have imagined that the war would drag on for another twenty months.

The Repatriation Problem

Rumors of the war's imminent end raised POWs' hopes to their highest level yet. But when the rumors did not come true, it had a devastating effect on prisoners who had counted on going home in a matter of weeks. As the months dragged on and the truce talks kept breaking down, some men gave in to bitterness and depression. In some cases, they even lost the will to live. Ironically, the main stick-ing point to ending the war was the ex-change of POWs. What should have been a mutual release of prisoners became tan-gled up in national prestige and ideology.

The problem was what to do with the 132,000 Communist POWs interned in South Korea after their release. The Communists simply wanted all prisoners returned to their units. That was not acceptable to the United States because officials had learned that a substantial

Communist POWs held in South Korea are lined up to exercise. Many Communist POWs refused to return to their homelands after the Korean War ended.

percentage of the prisoners held by the UN, both North Korean and Chinese, wanted to remain in South Korea.

Most of the soldiers who did not want to return to Communist control had been unwilling participants in the war. Both the Chinese and the North Koreans had forced thousands of men into the army against their will. With good reason, those former soldiers did not wish to return to Communist control. They believed that if they were sent back to China or North Korea it was likely they would be severely punished or even executed. For President Truman, it was a matter of principle. He publicly announced that "we will not buy an armistice by turning over human beings for slaughter or slavery."[56]

His stand, while an honorable one, helped keep the war going for almost two more years and greatly decreased his popularity in the United States. It also caused many American POWs to wonder whether their country had forgotten them. U.S. Army enlistee Billy Joe Harris was captured in February 1951 and spent more than two and a half years in Camp Three. "I couldn't understand why it took so long," he recalled. "It doesn't take that long to win or lose a war."[57]

Germ Bombs?

Truman's stand also upset China and North Korea—particularly when they learned that at least 40,000 of the 132,000 military POWs in South Korea were refusing to return to Communist control. That represented a huge propaganda victory for the UN and it infuriated the Communists. In response, North Korea and China broke off the truce talks numerous times while stepping up their own propaganda efforts. The first hint of the Communist strategy occurred at the UN in February 1952 when the Russians accused the United States of using bullets filled with toxic gases. Then, Communist newspapers around the world printed stories about how U.S. airmen and soldiers were dropping bombs and firing artillery shells, respectively, filled with bacteria-infected insects and rats on North Korea. Demonstrations, riots, and protest meetings followed. In order to prove these claims, the Communists released photos of special germ hunters picking up disease-carrying flies with chopsticks. They even claimed that the United States had developed a special kind of housefly to withstand the frigid Korean winters.

Next the Communists put extreme pressure on captured U.S. Air Force and Marine Corps pilots to "confess" on film and in press interviews that they had been part of a massive germ warfare campaign. Eventually, thirty-six fliers signed germ warfare confessions. Marine major Roy Bley was one of them. Shot down in 1952, he at first refused to admit to germ warfare. His Chinese captors then placed him in a lice-infested cave and forced him to sit at attention in the mud day after day. He also had to sleep on the mud floor. During frequent interrogations he had to

Bug Bombers

Harry J. Middleton, author of *The Compact History of the Korean War*, wrote this summary of the propaganda campaign begun early in 1952 to get the world to believe that the United States was involved in germ warfare:

> Captured American airmen were set upon by relays of Communist interrogators. They were threatened with death and punishment, with never seeing their homes and families again. They were tortured in ingenious ways, subjected to cold and hunger, kept in close and solitary confinement; and always they were questioned, hour upon hour, endlessly. As Dr. Charles Mayo eventually was to describe it, they were victims of "a method obviously calculated . . . to bring a man to the point where a dry crust of bread or a few hours uninterrupted sleep is a great event in his life . . . "

By May the Communists had what they wanted: the "confessions" of two of the airmen—both officers and pilots—that they had dropped infected insects over North Korea. Said one, in a statement which rang around the world: "The capitalist Wall Street warmongers in their greed, their ruthless greed, have caused this horrible crime of bacteriological warfare in order to get more money for themselves in hopes of spreading the war."

stand at attention until he fell from exhaustion. Guards would then kick or beat him with rifle butts until he got up.

After months of this kind of treatment the Chinese pronounced him a war criminal and told him that he would be sent to China for execution. For five straight days after his sentence, Bley was made to stand at attention in a cell so cold that its walls and floor were coated with ice. Forced to go for ninety-six hours without sleep and with frostbite numbing his feet and hands, Bley reached the limits of his endurance. "At the end of about five nights," he said, "I was pretty well mentally and physically broken."[58] Shown the confession of another pilot who had been similarly mistreated, Bley saw no reason to continue his resistance and "admitted" his role in the germ warfare campaign.

So did marine pilot and colonel Frank Schwable. Unrelenting cold, along with endless interrogations, illness, loneliness, and systematic degradation reduced him to the point where he invented a confession that was extremely detailed. "They say black is white, you say it is not," he recalled. "But you wind up agreeing."[59]

After months of this kind of coercion, the Chinese usually got exactly the statements they wanted. They made sure the confessions were increasingly detailed to increase suspicions that the United States might really be using germ warfare. Like most POWs, Don Poirot, an artilleryman in the U.S. Air Force who spent most of the war in Camps Two and Five, thought the germ warfare charges were laughable. But he knew of five young pilots who had "confessed" to germ warfare and he knew that

Report from a Torture Chamber

Philip Deane, who was a correspondent for the *London Observer*, was taken prisoner by the North Koreans. They tied him to a chair and tortured him for weeks in an attempt to get him to condemn American "atrocities." In his book, *I Should Have Died,* Deane vividly describes the state of mind reached by POWs tortured to the brink of death:

"Why not be reasonable? You agree that I want to help you. You agree that you want me to help you. Why won't you promise to broadcast?" . . . I forgot how many times this happened. It seemed to be happening often, though I do not know over what length of time. . . .

Eventually I had my last lucid moment. I was . . . no longer on the chair, no longer naked. I was, I think, on a bed, but I felt in-substantial. I can only compare the feeling to being drugged heavily with morphia. Nothing seemed precise. There were no distinct ends or beginning to objects. All was a cloud. And I felt very small physically, as if there were very little of me left. From far away I could hear Lavrenti and Kim [a Russian physician and a North Korean interrogator] talking. But their words were blurred. I knew I was at the end of my endurance. I made the firm decision to give in and I knew clearly what I was doing: I was going to broadcast whatever they wanted. And I knew that after that broadcast, there would be other things they would want me to do and I would do them. I felt immense relief, even joy. Then Lavrenti said: "He is dying. We must stop. We'll try other methods when he regains his strength."

the manner in which those confessions were obtained was no laughing matter:

They admitted to everything under the sun, up to but not including the crucifixion of Christ. My heart went out to those poor guys. If you had something that the enemy wanted, he got it. . . . When the Chinese finished with them, they told everything they knew and some things they didn't know. I was always thankful that I was just an artilleryman. I didn't have anything they needed.[60]

Bugs, Rats, and Riots

The Communists also put a great deal of effort into convincing the American POWs that their own government was using germ warfare. In Camp One, U.S. Army private first class Donald Elliot recalled about six weeks of classes about germ warfare followed by an exhibit of bugs, bomb fragments, and pictures. Afterwards, the men were given a written test to see how much they had "learned." They did so poorly that the Chinese gave up the idea of trying to convince them.

Like the prisoners in Camp One, most POWs considered the charges of germ warfare ridiculous. In another camp, prisoners taunted their guards by fitting a dead rat with a tiny parachute and then hanging it on a fence where the guards would find it in the morning. One POW caused an uproar when he grabbed some of the "deadly bugs" that were part of an exhibit and started eating them.

Around the time the first germ warfare charges were being made, the Communists opened another propaganda front. They purposely allowed trained agents to be captured so that they would be sent to POW camps run by the UN in South Korea. Once inside, they organized prisoner riots in February and March of 1952. As they had hoped, the riots were put down with force and the Communists used the incidents to mount a worldwide protest against the "inhumane" treatment in UN prisons.

The riots and charges of germ warfare complicated and delayed the truce talks going on at Panmunjom. Still, by the summer of 1952 the two sides were close to reaching agreement on an armistice line.

Soldiers treat wounded Communist POWs following a riot at a UN camp. Communist leaders organized such riots to convince the world that the UN treated its prisoners inhumanely.

But the repatriation problem remained a sticking point. Another frustrating year of negotiations followed before it was finally resolved.

Surviving the Bad Times

With the talks dragging on for months, then years, frustrated POWs began to wonder whether their government had forgotten them. Most were unaware of the worldwide propaganda war being waged around them. Maintaining a positive outlook was crucial, but it became harder and harder. Army enlistee Nick Tosques, a prisoner in Camp One, recalled moments of despair:

> There were times when I did lose hope of ever getting back. . . . They would get us in formation on the parade field and tell us the talks were going well, and we'd think, "Great, another month and we're out of here." Then they would get us out there a month or two later and tell us that the talks had broken down, that the Americans didn't want peace and that we were never going home.[61]

After this happened three or four times, some men became extremely depressed. With no end in sight, keeping up morale became critical. One of the best morale boosters was humor. Robert Schaefer recalled a POW at Camp One with an incredible memory for jokes. A salesman before the war, he entertained fellow prisoners with a new joke every day for twenty-eight months. Army sergeant Jerry Morgan, one of a group of African Americans segregated at Camp Five, agreed that laughter was priceless. All ten of the men in his squad survived the war—a fact that he credited to their upbeat attitude:

> "We were always laughing and talking and singing. The Chinese just couldn't comprehend that. We had them completely befuddled . . . and there we were acting foolish. I say foolish in the eyes of the Chinese, but to us this was a means of survival."[62]

Friendships also helped POWs through the hard times; though, according to U.S. Army sergeant first class Harley Coon, a man had to be careful of becoming too dependent on anyone else. If a close friend or two died, then it became harder for the survivor to go on. The men who did the best were not exactly loners—they were willing to help others—yet they kept some emotional distance.

Religion helped some POWs survive the worst times. James Thompson of the U.S. Army, a prisoner in Camp Five, had a deathly fear of being enclosed in tight spaces. Yet he survived the panic he felt when he was thrown into a hole in the ground for two weeks in the summer of 1952. "On about the fifth day, I found a peculiar strength in an old spiritual that I had sung so many times as a child," Thompson remembered. "I would start singing it each time I felt my resolve weakening."[63]

Sergeant Eugene Inman, who lost 135 pounds during his captivity, became a minister after the war. In the spring of 1953 he engineered a minor miracle by somehow convincing officials at Camp Four to allow him to hold church services. Inman recalled how there were tears in the eyes of the men as they sang hymns and read from the Bible. Many of them, no doubt, had long been praying for freedom. Later that summer those prayers would be answered.

☆ Chapter 5 ☆

A Bittersweet Freedom

During the spring and summer of 1953 the political issues that had held up the release of the POWs were finally resolved. That meant that the long ordeal of those American prisoners held in North Korea was finally coming to an end. By that fall, most of them would be back home in the United States. Their return to freedom should have been an occasion for great joy, but the POWs' welcome home was tempered greatly by widespread suspicion that some of them had collaborated with the Communists and by the fact that the Korean War had become unpopular. Master Sergeant Robert Yancey, a veteran of the war, summed it up this way: "People did not think we had been fighting to preserve democracy—they thought we had done something wrong."[64]

Korea had been a frequent topic of debate during the presidential election of 1952. By then the country had grown tired of a war that did not seem to be going anywhere. As the total number of American dead and wounded approached and then passed one hundred thousand, the border between North and South Korea was roughly in the same place as it had been when the war started. In the opinion of many historians, Republican candidate and World War II hero General Dwight D. Eisenhower won the presidency when he vowed to "concentrate on the job of ending the Korean War."[65] Not long after defeating Illinois governor Adlai Stevenson in the November election, Eisenhower visited Korea as he had promised during the campaign. He came away convinced that the war must end soon but unsure of how to bring about a truce. The talks at Panmunjom had been going on for a year and a half with no end in sight.

Then, suddenly, in late March 1953, surprising news reached Washington, D.C. Communist negotiators at Panmunjom had unexpectedly agreed to a token exchange of sick and wounded prisoners. They also strongly suggested that they were ready to seek a final solution to the war. Two major reasons have been suggested for their dramatic change of heart. First, the Chinese were tiring of the war and its enormous cost in money and manpower. Second, the death of Soviet premier Joseph Stalin earlier in the month had caused Communist Party leaders to be less interested in global expansion and more concerned with internal power struggles.

Time for a Trade

Whatever the reason, American officials were gratified to finally be able to negotiate the return of some of their long-suffering

Medics carry an injured American POW at Freedom Village during Operation Little Switch.

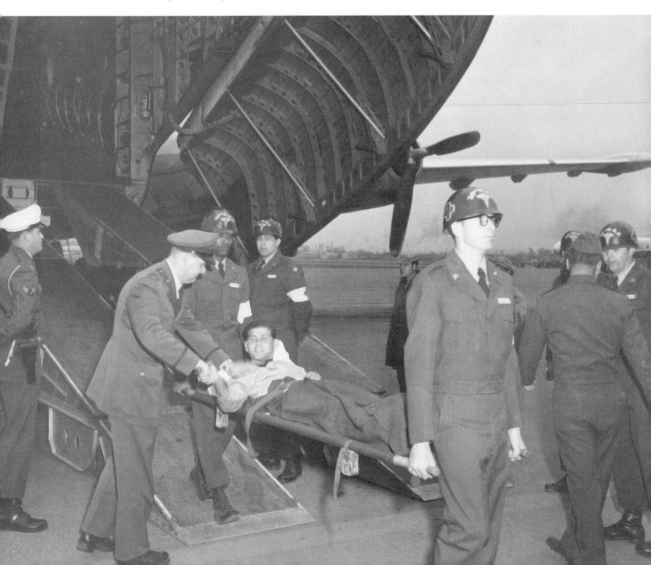

POWs. The exchange was to take place in two phases: Operation Little Switch followed by Operation Big Switch after the truce was signed. The first exchange began at Panmunjom on April 20, 1953, and continued until May 3. A group of doctors and nurses waited on the UN side of the line with ambulances ready to take ailing POWs fifteen miles south to a welcoming area that had been dubbed Freedom Village. Of the 684 UN prisoners released during Little Switch, 149 were Americans.

A few miles to the north, nearly ten times as many Communist prisoners were also being released. As newsreels filmed the scene they shouted their defiance at UN troops. In contrast, the American POWs were generally reluctant to talk about anything but the men they had left behind. There were two reasons for their silence. Among the first prisoners released were a number who appeared in surprisingly good health. The Communists had slipped a number of progressives into the ranks of the sick and wounded. They hoped that the condition of these POWs would convince the world how humane their prison camps were. The progressives, understandably, were not eager to explain why they were so well fed. Meanwhile, POWs who were truly sick and wounded refrained from talking publicly about how bad conditions were because they did not want to jeopardize the chances of future prisoner releases. They knew that the Communists might, as they had done so many times before, suddenly call off further negotiations.

News Too Good to Ignore

In the spring of 1953, while the negotiations that led to the Little Switch were going on, POWs in the camps had hints that their situation might be changing. In Camp Five an official called all the POWs into formation one day and told them of Stalin's death. The reaction, however, was not what he had hoped. "Immediately, without any thought," recalled Sergeant Donald Slagle, "we all raised our arms and cheered."[66] The official then went into a rage and put everyone to work hauling heavy rocks from place to place.

But that kind of punitive labor did not last long. POWs noticed a big change in the routines of Camp Five after March 1953. For the first time the Chinese began to show an interest in sanitation and cleanliness. Prisoners were allowed to take baths and encouraged to paint their quarters, mop and whitewash buildings, and even do a bit of landscaping. POW James Thompson recalled the sense that change was in the air:

> Rumors began to fly all over the place. First, the allies were knocking at the door. Next, peace talks were being considered. Finally, the rumor that we were going to be exchanged for enemy POWs. We began holding out for any hope. Ironically, the younger POWs stopped dying so fast.

The burial details were becoming less frequent. "Hope is eternal," someone once said. No lie. I can attest to that. Give a man hope and he will withstand things he would never consider withstanding earlier when there was no hope.[67]

What they saw in the skies overhead offered further hope for American POWs in the summer of 1953. Aerial dogfights between UN and Communist fighter planes had long been one of the few distractions available to prisoners. When all the planes stopped flying in late July it was an-other clue that the war might be winding down. On July 27, the day the armistice was signed, American fighter jets roared over some of the camps only thirty feet off the ground, waggling their wings to let the POWs know that the fighting had ended and that they had not been forgotten.

POWs at Camp Five had been reading about the possibility of an armistice in the

General Mark W. Clark (left) signs the armistice ending the Korean War. After the armistice was signed, treatment of POWs improved greatly.

Chinese-edited newspapers they received. So, when they were assembled for an announcement before news cameras on the twenty-seventh, they knew what it was going to be about. They had agreed beforehand not to show any emotion when the camp commandant told them that they would be released in several weeks. UN POWs did not want the Communists to use prisoners' supposed joy as further propaganda, perhaps to convince the world how humanely they had been treated.

Preparing for Release

By the time the armistice was signed in July, POWs definitely received better treatment. The reason was that a wave of revulsion had swept the Western world after Operation Little Switch. It was clear then that numerous prisoners had wounds that had never been treated and that many oth-

ers had been starved or psychologically mistreated. The Communists realized that the images of emaciated and brutalized men belied their claims of taking good care of their POWs. Thereafter, they began taking better care of their prisoners. Jeff Erwin recalled efforts to fatten men in the final weeks before their release:

By that time we had gotten rid of all of our lice, they had given us some cotton underwear, some blue clothing, and they improved conditions a great deal. We got two old scroungy pigs a week just loaded with a germ called trichinosis, a little white thing that looks like a louse, so we had to boil them—and boil them for hours in rice—before we figured it was safe to eat it. But all the prisoners picked up weight there during those months.[68]

The Bridge of No Return

As former POW Billy Joe Harris explains in Lewis H. Carlson's *Remembered Prisoners of a Forgotten War,* when he learned he was about to be released, he took a moment to reflect on his two and a half years of captivity:

I thought back on my first day in Camp Three after we had been marching for over three months with little or no food and without ever once washing. That first day I went down to this little creek to wash myself and my clothes. I looked in the water, and I saw a face. I looked around to see who it was; well, it was me. I couldn't even recognize myself. . . . At my lowest I

probably weighed about one hundred pounds. . . .

They had a holding area just on the north side of the 38th Parallel. They held us there and took so many of us each day in exchange for so many of theirs. I don't remember the exact date I was exchanged, but I do remember when my bunch crossed the Bridge of No Return, we threw away everything we had except our shorts. They ran us through a shower and gave us new clothes. They also offered us a cup of ice cream or a glass of milk. It was like a dream. We just couldn't believe we were free.

On the morning of August 5, a few days after the armistice was signed, Operation Big Switch began. The plan was to handle about four hundred prisoners a day, a process that would take about a month. In early August the Chinese began to empty the prison camps, putting POWs on trucks and trains headed south. The journey took several days. In some cases the POWs had been told where they were going. In other cases they had not. But even those who had been told still had

UN soldiers at Inchon watch Communist POWs being moved from UN landing ship tanks to trains during Operation Big Switch.

their doubts. "They had to keep repeating it," remembered Nick Tosques, "because by this time we didn't trust anything they said."[69]

Mind Games

Some men suspected they were simply being transferred to another camp and this was all just another Communist trick to break their morale. But as the trains and trucks kept moving south, the POWs' hopes inevitably began to rise. They eventually arrived in a holding area on the Communist side of the line north of Freedom Village. There they waited for several days until their turn came to be repatriated. While the POWs waited, the Communists had time for one last round of particularly cruel mental torture.

Both before and after the trucks began heading south, the Communists separated groups of POWs from those being released. They informed these men that they had been convicted of being war criminals and therefore would not be going home. Thompson nearly collapsed from disappointment when it was explained that he was being given a two-and-a-half-year sentence for his crimes against the North Korean people. "There was no way for me to mentally survive two and a half additional years in that place," he recalled. "No way!"[70]

Thompson was among a group of thirty-three POWs who were accused of being war criminals. The men were told they could not begin serving their time until the war was officially over. After the almost unbearable ordeal of seeing everyone else they knew go home, they, too, were finally released. At Panmunjom the Communists tried the same ploy with First Lieutenant William Funchess. Heartsick when he saw that his name was not on the list of prisoners to be exchanged,

he was stunned to learn that the reason was that, according to the Chinese, he was not a POW—he was a war criminal.

The Communists used such maneuvers for propaganda purposes and as simple harassment. In some cases they succeeded in coercing desperate POWs to sign one last false confession in return for being allowed to go free. Although Funchess did not give the Communists, what they wanted, he was eventually released. Since neither he nor Thompson had been good students of communism, their treatment may have been simple retaliation for their reactionary behavior in the camps. Whatever the reason, Funchess and Thompson were among those most relieved to reach the safety of Freedom Village.

Private First Class Wayne Johnson, the soldier who compiled a secret list of nearly five hundred dead POWs, had a special reason for breathing a huge sigh of relief when he left Communist territory. In the final days before their release the Chinese issued POWs new clothing and allowed them to shower and shave while they waited their turn to be repatriated. The men were even given toothpaste from the Red Cross. Johnson, still in possession of his list, realized he was in grave danger if it were discovered. So, with guards standing only ten feet away, he peeled open a toothpaste tube and hid the rolled up names inside. The trick worked and he and his priceless list made it safely to Freedom Village.

"We Almost Lost You Guys"

Glenn Reynolds was with a group of over two hundred POWs who were just a few miles north of Panmunjom and freedom on September 4, 1953. But as Reynolds recalls in Lewis H. Carlson's book, *Remembered Prisoners of a Forgotten War*, they had one last gut-wrenching experience to endure:

> That afternoon, they loaded us up on trucks and drove us out the front gate. But instead of turning south, where we should have been going, the trucks turned north. We quickly knew that we were heading toward China and not the 38th parallel. We decided they were planning to keep us so we planned to jump the guards. We realized that some of us would get killed, but we decided we had to risk it and take the vehicles and make a run for the 38th parallel. About thirty minutes later, the drivers pulled over to the side of the road and put us in a rice paddy. . . . Then they put us back on the trucks and turned around and drove back to the staging area. The next morning they loaded us up again, but this time they headed south [to Freedom Village]. . . .

> A fellow prisoner named Forrest Montgomery had a brother Roy with the United Nations' command. He was waiting for Forrest to come through, and he told us, "We almost lost you guys. Yesterday, the chief UN negotiator, General [William] Harrison, asked the People's Liberation Army's chief negotiator when they were going to release the rest of their prisoners." When they denied having any, Harrison said, "You've got about six hundred up there. You keep them and we'll keep the thousands we've got." Harrison then got up and walked out. There were still thousands of Communist prisoners waiting to be repatriated to the north. That's the reason they stopped our trucks. So we got out of there by the skin of our teeth.

Freedom Village

Set up near the town of Munsan, some fifteen miles south of Panmunjom, Freedom Village was a cluster of tents centered around an old army warehouse converted into a hospital. It was the scene of many emotional moments. After crossing the line at Panmunjom, POWs were taken by ambulance to Munsan. One of the conditions of the peace agreement was the establishment of a neutral zone consisting of several hundred yards between the Communist side of the line and the South Korean side. Each prisoner had to walk across the line on his own to prove that he wanted to be repatriated. Between August 5 and September 6, some 12,773 UN prisoners, including 3,597 Americans, made the walk to freedom. Colonel William Thrash recalled how, at the end of their journey, the men strained to catch the first sight of the American flag. "Normally," he recalled, "you don't think much about it, but when you spend a couple of years without seeing it, you surely do miss it."[71]

At the end of their walk to freedom, the POWs were greeted by an American general and other officers who saluted them and shook their hands. Tosques was so excited when he jumped off the truck that brought him to the truce area that his trousers caught on a handle and ripped completely down the seam. He could not salute because he was holding up his pants. "Don't worry about that son," said a colonel. "Just get across that line."[72]

Richard Bassett never forgot his first moments of freedom:

As I walked across the line of freedom and entered the tent, another American officer shook my hand and said, "Welcome home, soldier." I was a free man, and my eyes filled with tears. . . . I was then escorted to a waiting ambulance that transported me to this dreamworld called Freedom Village. It was too wonderful and emotional an experience to put into words.[73]

A released American POW delivered to Freedom Village is helped from a truck.

Released American POWs sit down to a healthy meal in Freedom Village. Many POWs had difficulty adjusting to normal eating habits following their captivity.

Like Bassett, a number of prisoners broke into tears when they first saw the American flag and realized they were free at last. After the ride to Freedom Village they were given haircuts, showers, medical checks, and their first decent meal. Private First Class Donald Elliott greatly enjoyed the roast beef, mashed potatoes, corn, bread and butter, and apple pie with ice cream, but two of his teeth were so infected that his jaw swelled up after-

ward. Most of the POWs had difficulty adjusting to normal food. Staff Sergeant Thomas Gaylets asked for a chocolate milk shake but became sick as soon as it hit his stomach. Tosques piled his tray high with food, but could only manage a couple of bites. After two and a half years of imprisonment POWs' digestive systems were in such poor shape that it would be months, and for some, years, before they could eat a normal meal.

Some of the men were so excited by their freedom that they could not sleep for a couple of days, but a surprising number seemed to have difficulty comprehending their status. Lieutenant Gough Reinhart was part of the Big Switch team welcoming POWs. He was struck by the number of men who displayed little emotion. "They've had so many disappointments they won't let themselves accept it—they think there must be a catch somewhere."[74]

An inability to show happiness was so common that army psychiatrists came up with a nickname for the condition. They called it the "Zombie Reaction."[75] Like the survivors of Nazi death camps during World War II, some Korean War POWs had been so brutalized that they had trouble learning how to express normal emotions again.

Testing for Loyalty

The subdued reactions of some brutalized POWs only helped raise the level of suspicion they all would face in the months and years to come. Unlike in previous wartime these men would not be greeted as returning heroes. Instead, they immediately underwent psychiatric testing and intense interrogations that, for many, seemed distressingly similar to the interrogations they had endured while held captive.

From Freedom Village the returning POWs were moved west to the port of Inchon. Most of them would be put aboard ships for the long voyage home. But first came a round of psychiatric testing by a team of forty-five psychiatrists and psychologists. The U.S. Army felt it needed to determine the mental condition of the returnees. The many publicized "confessions" of POWs during the war had raised concerns that these men might have been brainwashed or even become Communist agents.

Suspicions were further aroused by the stunning news that twenty-three Americans had chosen not to be repatriated. Back in the United States people wondered how anyone could freely choose communism over democracy. The actions of these twenty-three "turncoats" seemed to confirm the worst fears about Communist brainwashing. In truth, the defectors chose to stay behind for mostly personal reasons rather than a true love of communism.

Some were progressives who feared retribution for their less-than-honorable behavior in the camps once they returned to the United States. Others, like army corporal Edward Dickenson, gave in to threats by the Chinese. He was told that if he did not consider staying with the Communists they would send all the recordings and articles they had forced him to make back to the U.S. government and they would undoubtedly sentence him to prison for collaborating with the enemy.

Always mindful of the propaganda value, the Communists offered inducements to other POWs to get them to stay. Clarence Adams, one of three black men who refused repatriation, had suffered severe racism while growing up in the South. The Chinese promised him a college education if he stayed in China and he accepted their offer. Whatever the reason they decided to stay, all but one of the "turncoats" would eventually leave China.

On the Spot Again

However, their actions, coming at the height of the Cold War, shocked Americans at home and cast a pall of suspicion over all POWs returning from Korea. That suspicion was evident in the arrangements aboard the ships that brought the POWs back to the United States. Each ship carried about 350 men, but before the men were loaded onto the boats, carpenters built dozens of booths inside the ships. Only about four feet by four feet, the booths had room for a small desk and two chairs. During the two-week voyage back to America, the ships became floating interrogation centers. POWs were questioned for hours at a time by the Counter Intelligence Corps (CIC) of the army.

Sergeant First Class Harley Coon did not have pleasant memories of those interviews. He was questioned eight hours a day for fifteen days. Sergeant Eugene

Inman experienced deep feelings of anger, anxiety, and distrust aboard ship. He had expected a thorough medical exam to deal with his physical problems. "Instead," he recalled, "I was pushed through the exam, placed on a helicopter and sent aboard a slow ship to the States. Slow, because they spent most of the time picking our brains."[76]

The interrogators mostly wanted to know who had collaborated, but it was clear that everyone was under suspicion. They had a list of seventy questions that they asked over and over again. It all left a bad feeling in the mind of Robert Jones, a POW who had miraculously survived in Camp Five after being given up for dead. "Those Americans interviewing us after we were liberated never seemed to be that interested in our wounds or diseases. They really weren't interested in a damn thing except did we collaborate."[77]

Johnson's interrogation aboard ship was similarly unsettling. During his interview on the ship going home, the moment he had long been waiting for arrived. He was asked whether he knew the names of any of the prisoners who died. At that point, he pulled out his list of 496 names and began recording them. But he had gotten only a few of the names written down, when an officer dismissed him, telling him that it would take too long. For the next thirty-six years, no one in the military showed the slightest interest in the list that he had compiled at the risk of his life.

Homecoming

The interrogations finally ended when the ships reached California. The first of many joyous reunions took place there, although most POWs would discover that their welcome by the rest of the nation would be short-lived. Slagle recalled the moment he had been waiting for since his capture nearly three years earlier:

> We went under the Golden Gate and docked in San Francisco. They called our names, and we departed the ship. My folks were there, my brother Ernie and his wife, and my cousin Don Young. I was so happy to see them. . . . We drove to a café and went in to eat. Ernie ordered me a steak, but I told him I couldn't eat it. My stomach had shrunk so much, it didn't take much at all to fill it up.[78]

While POWs like Slagle had tearful reunions with their loved ones in San Francisco, many others had to wait until they arrived at their hometowns. When army sergeant Walter Adelman arrived at the airport in Lockport, Illinois, he was escorted into town by two motorcycle cops, given a parade, and handed the key to the city. Despite Adelman's dramatic homecoming, most POWs found that they were returning to a country that had tired of the Korean War. Few people wanted to be reminded of a conflict that some were claiming was the first war that America had lost. "When I came home everybody was happy and all excited to

An American POW hugs family members during a joyous reunion. Adjusting to a normal life back home was difficult for most POWs.

see me, and it lasted for two or three days,"[79] recalled Coon.

Coon and Adelman and most of the other Korean War POWs discovered that after so many years without freedom, their adjustment to normal life was not going to be easy. At the time all they wanted to do was get home as fast as possible. Only years later did they realize that they should have had some kind of counseling to help them make the transition to civilian life. Billy Joe Harris, who was from Missouri, was one of those who later wished it would have been different:

One thing I have against the government to this day was its lack of any kind of program to help us readjust to normal life. Of course, I didn't realize it at the time because all I wanted to do was get out and get home—and I did . . . I was just turned loose. It was really hard on me because I didn't even know how to act around other people.[80]

79

Chapter 6

Legacy of an Unpopular War

Korean War POWs faced a multitude of problems once they had returned home. The physical and mental effects of their imprisonment lingered for decades. Meanwhile, the untrue but widespread suspicion that the majority of POWs either had been brainwashed or had collaborated with the Communists caused deep-seated resentments that hindered the healing process. The country seemed to be doing its best to forget the Korean War and the men who fought it. Not until four decades later would a national memorial be built for those who fought there. Its dedication signaled a long overdue appreciation for the sacrifices of Korean War POWs.

But when the POWs returned home in the summer and fall of 1953, memorializing the conflict was not a priority for anyone. The Korean War was widely seen as the first battle of the Cold War and both the media and the military were concerned with assessing blame for what

many regarded as a defeat for democracy. When the U.S. Army court-martialed thirteen former Korean War POWs in 1954 and 1955, it was the first time in history that American POWs were charged with collaborating with the enemy.

Although three of the men were acquitted, the trials were widely criticized by many Americans who felt the former prisoners were being made scapegoats for the country's military and political failures. In a letter to President Eisenhower, Mildred Fontano, a woman from Alameda, California, expressed a common sentiment:

How much does a soldier for the United States have to endure? Have you looked at the pictures of those prisoners of war? The haggard thin flesh, the hollow haunted vacant eyes? Oh, God, have mercy on us and help us as a nation to not heap any more indignities on suffering humanity and especially on our own loved ones.[81]

Others, however, were much less forgiving. They saw POW behavior in Korea as evidence of what was wrong with America. Some of the most vocal critics claimed that the conduct of American POWs proved the "weakness" of the American fighting man. One of the foremost proponents of this point of view was army major William E. Mayer. In magazine articles and on nationwide lecture tours he maintained that the behavior of POWs in Korean prison camps fell far short of the historical American standards of honor, character, loyalty, courage, and personal integrity. Mayer contended that the harsh treatment POWs received could not explain their susceptibility to what he called brainwashing. Instead he blamed their behavior on domineering mothers who weakened their sense of discipline, teachers who did not provide young men with the basics of democracy, and the U.S. Army for its softness in training soldiers for war.

Blaming the Victim

The ideas of men like Mayer received a great deal of publicity in the years following the war. Meanwhile, POWs felt they were being blamed unfairly for their actions. Michael Cornwell spoke for many when he said:

Turncoat American POWs return to the United States to face military authorities for collaborating with the enemy.

A guy by the name of William Mayer wrote about the alleged misbehavior of the Korean War POWs, and there's not a POW who isn't thoroughly unhappy with what this guy wrote. I'd like to put Mayer in those camps for a while. According to him we were all collaborators, but that's just not true. I don't think Americans in any war have ever faced what we did. You look at the conditions, you look at what we didn't have. What would you expect?[82]

Another man who was highly unpopular with POWs was journalist Eugene Kinkead. In an influential book, *In Every War but One*, he contended that American POWs in Korea had disgraced themselves as never before. According to Kinkead, nearly one out of every three prisoners collaborated with the Communists. And he claimed that the vast majority passively cooperated in indoctrination and interrogation sessions. He blamed both the high level of collaboration and the high death rate in the camps on prisoners' personal and cultural shortcomings while minimizing the brutal conditions.

Gaunt UN POWs relax following their release. Some Americans condemned POWs for their behavior after being tortured.

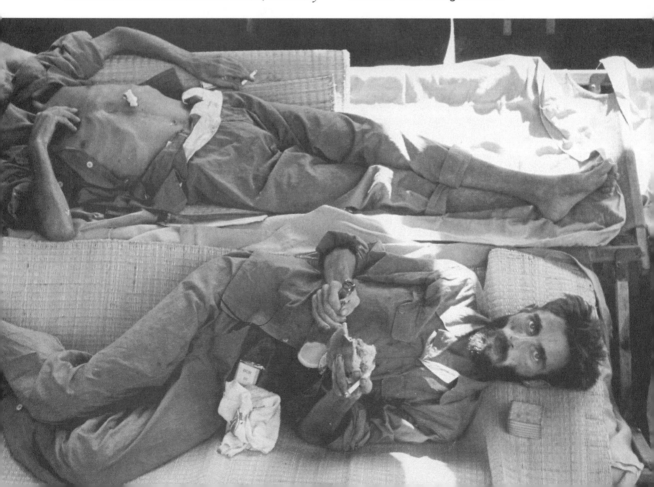

Captured American Soldiers

Out of 1.6 Million in Korean Conflict 7,190 Were Captured

An Additional 470 Were Missing

- 21 refused repatriation
- 11 retained by the Communists against their will but subsequently released

2,730 DEAD

4,428 ALIVE

7,190 CAPTURED

Army	👤👤👤👤👤👤👤👤👤	93%
Air Force	👤	3%
Marine Corps	👤	3%
Navy	👤	1%

Prepared by Defense Advisory Committee on Prisoners of War

Like William Mayer, Kinkead deplored the "weakness" of American POWs. He compared them unfavorably with the 229 Turkish POWs in Korea who endured their captivity with no loss of life. While Turkish soldiers certainly adjusted to imprisonment better than other UN prisoners, there were extenuating circumstances. According to Kinkead, they were elite, professional soldiers and it was probably unfair to compare them with Americans, many who had been unwilling draftees or reservists. Kinkead also downplayed the fact that most of the Turks were captured after the deadly winter of 1950–1951 when camp conditions had begun to improve. But perhaps most important of all, they never had to endure month after month of indoctrination. Since the Chinese had no "educators" who spoke Turkish, they had little success in breaking down their group solidarity.

In essence, both Kinkead and Mayer were saying that what happened in the camps was due more to the flawed character of American soldiers and airmen than the brutal conditions of their imprisonment. They claimed that too many of these men were soft, though others have pointed out that, having grown up during the depression, the soldiers in Korea were among the least pampered generation in history.

Regardless, that kind of thinking was reflected in dozens of magazine articles written during the 1950s. These articles had titles like "Washed Brains of POWs: Can They Be Rewashed?"; "Why POWs Collaborate"; and "Cowardice in Korea." A story in the January 26, 1959, issue of *Newsweek* entitled "Why G.I.'s Folded," had the unsettling news that "Seventy-five men . . . returned to the U.S. as trained agents of Communist espionage. Some of these men, not having committed any overt act, are still living ostensibly as legitimate American citizens."[83] Read by millions of Americans, such articles, which also appeared in popular magazines like *Time* and *Life*, fostered widespread suspicion of returning POWs. For POWs themselves, they only triggered more feelings of defensiveness, guilt, and anger.

Still, one award-winning movie probably did more to tarnish the image of returning POWs than all the negative magazine articles combined. Winner of the Academy Award in 1962, *The Manchurian Candidate* was a tense, political thriller. The movie told the story of Sergeant Raymond Shaw, a POW who had been brainwashed by his Chinese and Russian captors, then programmed to murder the president of the United States. It was a gripping but unsettling film with an unforgettable portrait of an American POW reduced to the status of a mindless killer. In one memorable line from the movie Shaw's handlers brag that his "brain has not only been washed, it has been dry-cleaned."[84] The film was so disturbing that it was taken out of circulation after President Kennedy was assassinated. By then, its distorted picture of brainwashed prisoners had become part of American popular culture.

The Questioning Continues

In addition to all the movies, books, and magazine articles casting them in a negative light, many Korean War POWs found themselves subjected to continuing interrogations. Years after their return to the United States, investigators from the mili-

In a scene from The Manchurian Candidate, *Frank Sinatra (second from left) sits with fellow POWs during an indoctrination session.*

tary, the CIA, and the FBI were still trying to get POWs to inform on each other as to who might be a Communist sympathizer. The fact that, after all they had gone through, their own government did not trust them made many former POWs bitter and resentful.

For Lieutenant Colonel Charles Fry it was all too much: "The tribulations and trials that all the ex-POWs have been through, the interrogations—I have spent more hours on the interrogations than on duty since I've been back from Korea and in fact, it motivated my early retirement from the service to try and get away

from it."[85] Army sergeant Donald Slagle was visited so many times by CIA agents that he finally had to order them to leave him alone because he was trying to forget the past and start a new life.

A Justifiable Anger

While accusations of cowardice and collaboration embittered Korean War POWs, more positive assessments of their behavior received far less public notice. Many

POWs felt such a deep resentment about the charges leveled against them that they had difficulty getting on with their lives. Peggy Himmelheber, a psychiatric nurse who works with former POWs, explains why Korean War prisoners have had a particularly difficult time coming to terms with their past:

> I think the biggest thing is the disservice that was done to them by our own government after they came home. There was such a big hullabaloo about how these individuals were lesser men than those from World War II, and that the country was in shambles with no moral standards. Critics such as Kinkead and Mayer really put the blame on them, saying that they were less patriotic, more pampered and had less stamina and integrity than previous POWs. They derided them and blamed them for not being able to hold up, when in fact they held up just as well as anyone else.[86]

Studies made after Kinkead's book appeared support Himmelheber's claim. In 1962 a group of scholars published a paper entitled "Statement: To Set Straight the Korean POW Episode." They concluded that, compared with other wars, instances of moral weakness and collaboration with the enemy occurred no more frequently in Korea. Albert D. Biderman's 1963 book, *March to Calumny*, also disputed the notion that Korean War POWs were somehow flawed.

In his book, *The Captives of Korea*, William Lindsay White strongly denied that an alarmingly high percentage of American POWs had disgraced themselves. He contended that the number one reason so many American POWs died was the lack of food and medical supplies. He emphasized that our prisoners were treated with a savagery never before seen in modern times and also disputed the notion that the decision of the twenty-one American "turncoats" to remain behind represented a huge propaganda victory for communism. After all, of the more than 171,000 prisoners held in South Korea, only 83,000 freely chose to return to Communist control (and half of those probably just wanted to return to their families). Unfortunately, supportive statements like those made by White and Biderman never received the same degree of publicity that the negative ones did. If they had, they might have helped POWs deal with the anger and guilt many were experiencing.

A Tough Adjustment

The resentment felt by many POWs was just one of many factors complicating their difficult adjustment to life after imprisonment. Heavy drinking was common among former prisoners as men turned to alcohol to help them deal with painful memories. Trying to forget Korea, Sergeant Walter Adelman drank for two months straight. Years later, he wrote a letter to a newspaper eloquently describing the plight of so many former POWs:

To be a prisoner of war is to suffer the agony of rehabilitation in a suddenly alien world. It is the frustration of trying to cope and fit into a society that seems foreign and unable to relate to your experiences.

It is the resentment you immediately feel for those who have never felt what you have, seen what you have, and whose personal problems pale by comparison. It is the recurring nightmares that will plague you for the rest of your days. It is the nagging question, "What was it all for? What good did it do? Who cares?"[87]

To this day, nightmares, sleep problems, and irritability are very common among Korean War POWs. Although the cluster of medical problems that have come to be known as post-traumatic stress disorder (PTSD) were not even identified until after the Vietnam War, it seems clear now that many Korean War POWs suffer from it. A scene in a movie or a television show can remind them of Korea and cause them to relive the ordeal of their captivity with flashbacks, nightmares, and frightening thoughts. Here is the testimony of the wife of an ex-POW:

After all these years, I still hear him talking in his sleep. He'll be back in that POW camp. Maybe they've been sneaking out getting a potato or something. He'll say, "Hey, be quiet. They're coming. If they catch us, they'll shoot us." . . . You don't yell at him when he wakes up. Just last night I thought he was choking, but when I

They Fought for Freedom

In his 1995 book, *Witness to War: Korea*, U.S. Army colonel, combat veteran, and West Point instructor Rod Paschall makes the case that, despite all the negative media coverage afterwards, history has shown that the sacrifices of Korean War veterans were fully justified.

The Korean War remains America's most misunderstood and ill-analyzed conflict. Those who called it "the wrong war at the wrong place at the wrong time" failed to comprehend that the truly just wars are fought not because they are convenient, but because a failure to resist, a failure to fight, would be morally wrong. There are, quite simply, conditions worse than war.

Those who claimed the war to be the only one America had ever lost failed to acknowledge the conflict's actual results. An aggressor had been deprived of his unlawful gains, had been severely punished, and had his own territory reduced. Those who saw the war as a waste failed to see the war in its true light. The Korean War was the hot and bloody opening campaign of a global struggle misnamed the Cold War. . . . Both the Cold War and the Korean War were waged by the West on principles that proved more compelling, more worthy, and more enduring than those of its adversary. For the United States, the Korean War was fought for the right reasons.

tried to wake him up, he was ready for battle. I have to be very cautious because he's just as scared as I am.[88]

Many POWs also display the typical PTSD symptoms of emotional numbness, depression, anxiety, inability to concentrate, and outbursts of anger. Their suffering has been compounded by the fact that, unlike Vietnam-era veterans, these men grew up in a time when most men kept their feelings to themselves. It is often difficult for them to share their true feel-

ings with others. Even worse, some POWs were warned by military officials never to talk about their imprisonment after their release from the service. Since they could not or would not speak about what was troubling them, they rarely got the help they needed. Often, even their own families did not know what they were going through. Some former POWs, for exam-

Two amputees wait for artificial limbs in a hospital. Many POWs were left with severe physical reminders of their participation in the Korean War.

ple, never even told their wives that they had once been prisoners.

Reminders of a Painful Past

In addition to the mental burdens carried by former POWs, most have had to cope with physical reminders of Korea for the rest of their lives. The abuse and starvation that POWs suffered back then have caused a variety of long-term medical problems. Frostbite, nerve disorders, digestive problems, deteriorating eyesight, and cirrhosis of the liver are but a few of the maladies common to former prisoners. Billy Gaddy, for example, was punched and slapped in the head so often at Camp Three that he has suffered from excruciating headaches ever since. The malnutrition he endured causes painful stomach cramps and his left foot is in constant pain from barefoot marches he was forced to make in subzero temperatures.

According to statistics provided by the government, former prisoners also suffer from illnesses and diseases at a much higher rate than military veterans of the same age who were not POWs. The mental and physical battering they sustained in Korea seems to have caused lifelong health consequences. For example, one out of four former Korean War POWs develops heart disease, as compared to about one out of ten non-POWs. About 35 percent of POWs suffer from ulcers; only 4.5 percent of non-POWs do. And POWs get cancer at a rate almost thirteen times that of non-POWs.

In addition, POWs received remarkably little medical help from their own government in the first few decades after the war. For years, former prisoners tried to convince the Veterans Health Administration (VHA) that their long-term health problems could be traced back to their experiences in Korea. They had little luck until 1982, when Congress passed a POW bill that enabled them to get a physical examination to assess their condition. For some of the POWs it was the first military physical they had ever received. Former POW Bill Ashworth reports that he never had a physical before he went into the service nor did he when he got out. He ended up fighting with the VHA for four years before they finally granted him 100 percent disability for his experiences in Korea.

A New Understanding

Despite their battles with the VHA, most POWs would agree that the 1980s and 1990s saw a change for the better, both in their own attitudes and in the public's attitude toward them. Part of that change can be traced back to the welcome home received by Vietnam-era POWs after that Asian war. It also helped that people were beginning to see POWs in a more sympathetic light. In addition, the difficulties that Vietnam veterans had in returning to civilian life led to a more widespread understanding of the effects of post-traumatic stress, both among the public and among former POWs.

Thirty Years Too Late

More than forty years after the Korean War ended, veteran Jim Crombie was still bitter about the lack of medical care for returning POWs who were understandably in a hurry to get home and see their families. He explained why in *Remembered Prisoners of a Forgotten War* by Lewis H. Carlson:

> They did us a great disservice in that they did not make us sit down and tell them what was wrong with us when we came back. They could have started when we were on that ship for two weeks. Then we went to Fort Dix for a couple of days. All they asked was, "Are you feeling all right?"

"Yeah, man, I feel great. I want to go home."

"Well, okay. Is there anything else wrong with you?"

"No, I'm fine. I feel good. I don't have any hurts, nothing." Then, in 1983 they called us in for a physical protocol [examination] but that was thirty years after the fact. Then they asked, "Did you say anything about this when you got out?"

"Hell no, I wanted to get out. I wanted to get home. I didn't want to take a chance on going to a hospital." I ended up in a hospital anyhow for about a year and a half. But I mean everybody was like that. All the guys were the same way.

For the first time in their lives, many Korean War POWs began to realize the importance of talking with others about their experiences. As they discovered that their memories and afflictions were not so much something to be ashamed of as they were typical reactions to a traumatic experience, they began to feel better about themselves. Many experienced a newfound sense of pride. Meanwhile, the discussions they were having with others helped bring them out of their isolation. Charley Davis, who was incarcerated in Camp Five, attended his first Korean Ex-Prisoners of War Association reunion in Columbus, Ohio, in 1983. The meeting changed his whole attitude:

> Talking to those guys made me realize we were experiencing the same kinds of things. Before this, I thought I was

an oddball. I had nightmares all the time but couldn't remember them. My wife would tell me about them, but I still didn't remember a thing. That bothered me. Hearing that some of the other guys experienced the same thing made me feel a little better. I realized I wasn't crazy.[89]

Former POW Glenn Reynolds was extremely skeptical about the value of reliving his Korean experiences. He waited forty-four years before attending a meeting of POWs at his local VA hospital in 1997. Reluctant to say anything for the first couple of weeks, when he finally did open up he found, like many others before him, that the experience helped him to heal. Not long afterward, he sat down and wrote a history of what he had done in the military for his family. Since he had never spoken about Korea with them, they had no idea that he had won ten Bronze Stars. Their positive responses to his recollections convinced him that sharing his story was a helpful thing to do.

His Sacrifice Recognized at Last

Former artilleryman Wayne Johnson can also attest to the value of sharing memories with others. Like so many other POWs, his return to civilian life did not go smoothly. He was haunted by nightmares and turned to alcohol to ease the pain. Drifting from job to job, he was married and divorced four times. Finally, in the 1980s, after he was treated for post-traumatic stress disorder, Johnson began living a more normal life. Still, in all that time, no one showed any interest in the list he had compiled at the risk of his life.

That finally changed in 1989 when Johnson attended his first ex-POW reunion. Thirty survivors of the Tiger Death March gathered at a hotel in Evansville, Indiana. Their group was called the Tiger Survivors and at one point in the evening a dozen men were sitting around a table trying in vain to recall when a particular comrade had died. Then a newcomer spoke up. "I know *exactly* when,"[90] announced Johnson. He then went back to his room and retrieved his list. After scanning two and a half pages crammed with rows of printed names, he told the astonished men that the POW they were asking about had died in a frozen cornfield out-

side the town of Manpo just before the death march began.

Survivor Wilbert Estabrook, the organizer of the reunion, had been part of a group that had been trying for years to construct an accurate roster of POWs who had died during the Tiger Death March and afterward. "Your list is important, Johnnie,"[91] he declared. Johnson then agreed to help Estabrook figure out what had happened to men whose fate had been unclear for nearly forty years.

There were almost 500 names on Johnson's list, but residual toothpaste had caused one-fourth of them to fade to illegibility. With the help of an infrared scanner and a forensic document examiner the two men eventually recovered more than 100 of the previously illegible names. By the summer of 1991, the restored list was nearing the original 496 names. Checking the list against military records, Estabrook and Johnson were surprised to learn that most of the men were still officially classified as missing in action (MIA). There were also 147 POWs on Johnson's list that the Communists claimed had escaped from captivity. Although Johnson was certain that these men had died, privacy laws forbid the Pentagon from giving him the addresses of their families.

Still, word of his list spread and it began helping families. The father of Mary Lou Hoolihan of St. Cloud, Minnesota, was one of the men the Chinese claimed had escaped from captivity. Hoolihan could not help wondering whether he had been recaptured and held against his will after the war ended. She knew that he was probably dead, but there was always that slight chance that he was still being held somewhere. As with so many of the families of men classified as missing in action, the uncertainty was a form of mental torture.

In 1991 Hoolihan attended the Tiger Survivor reunion, which was held in Denver that year. She looked up Wayne Johnson, and anxiously told him the story of her dad. He sorted through his papers and found a photocopy of the list. Pointing to one of the columns, he showed her father's name followed by his date of death: 4-29-51. Now Hoolihan knew for sure that her father was not coming home. At first she began to cry, but then she experienced a tremendous sense of release. Knowing for sure what had really happened was a great comfort. Her reaction affected Johnson deeply. His eyes, too, filled with tears. "After 40 years I've been able to help one family," he said. "Risking my life was worthwhile."[92]

In the years that followed, Johnson helped other families put the past behind them. His work caught the attention of U.S. Army Reserve sergeant Victoria Bingham of the Defense Department's POW/MIA Office. She had heard about his list while attending a Korean Ex-POW Association reunion in Sacramento, California. Impressed by all the good the list was doing—and by the courage and determination that it took to create it—Bingham

started a campaign to have him awarded a medal for his sacrifices. She also helped to see that his list became part of the Defense Department's database for POWs and MIAs.

Finally, on August 3, 1996, Lieutenant General John E. Miller of the U.S. Army pinned a Silver Star, the nation's third-highest medal for valor, on Johnson's chest. Miller thanked Johnson for his "exemplary courage and selfless determination to provide a record of deceased soldiers, even in the face of death by a hostile enemy." Referring to those lonely years when Johnson seemed to be the only person in America who believed his list was important, Miller added, "I'm very glad to see you receive this award, even though it has taken a very long time for you to be recognized."[93] Recognition for Johnson, and indeed for all Korean War POWs, has been long in coming. Yet, for most of the surviving captives of that remarkably brutal war, the acclaim is better late than never.

A Memorial at Last

The growing pride of Korean POWs received a big boost on July 27, 1995, when the Korean War Veterans Memorial was dedicated in Washington, D.C. Until then, the Korean War was the only major war to not have its own national memorial. "The Korean War was the forgotten war," claimed ex-POW Wilfred Ruff. "The government just wanted to forget about us."[94] Ruff's attitude was shared by most Korean War veterans. All that changed when President Bill Clinton and South Korea's president Kim Young Sam dedicated the new memorial. Although the ceremony took place forty-two years after the fighting stopped, it was still the largest ever to honor the men who fought in Korea. And the many grateful Koreans who attended the ceremony made the day's events even more meaningful.

The memorial depicts nineteen infantrymen under attack moving up a slope. Off to the side is a polished granite wall etched with hundreds of ghostly faces. Nearby, a grove of linden trees and a reflecting pool recall all those taken prisoner, killed, or missing in action. Perhaps because of their four-decade wait for recognition, many former POWs found their first visit to the monument a deeply moving experience. Equally as fulfilling for these veterans was the parade down Constitution Avenue two days later. More than twenty thousand Korean War veterans participated. James Walsh, winner of three Purple Hearts in Korea, spoke for many when he called the weekend's events "the greatest thing I ever saw in my life, ever, ever."[95]

The growing appreciation of Korean War veterans has been reflected in new perspectives on the war and its aftermath. The collapse of communism in Eastern Europe in 1989 signaled the end of the

An American POW reportedly being held in Korea is pictured in a South Korean newspaper in 1996. Hundreds of UN POWs were still missing in action years after the Korean War ended.

Nineteen statues of infantrymen stand in Washington, D.C., as a memorial to those who fought in the Korean War. The memorial was dedicated forty-two years after the war ended.

Cold War and caused historians to reassess the Korean War. Long thought of as the first battle of the Cold War, it is no longer seen as a humiliating defeat. Instead, a Communist aggressor had been deprived of the territory it seized and severely punished. In his book, *Witness to War: Korea*, Rod Paschall summed up the new belief that the sacrifices made during the Korean War were ultimately worthwhile: "Both the Cold War and the Korean War were waged by the West on principles that proved more compelling, more worthy, and more enduring than those of its adversary."[96]

A Symbol of Gratitude

While regard for Korean War POWs has been increasing in recent years, advanced age and war-related maladies are taking a toll. The ranks of these men are dwindling every year. According to the Department of Veterans Affairs, an estimated 3.9 million veterans who served in the military during the Korean War were still alive in 2000. Those numbers were down from 1990 when there were almost 5 million. The number of Korean War POWs still alive is, of course, much smaller.

In 2001 those survivors and veterans who served in Korea received a pleasant surprise. In order to show its gratitude for their sacrifices, the South Korean government announced that it would begin issuing the Republic of Korea Korean War Service Medal. The medal came with a letter of appreciation from the South Korean government. One of the first presentations was made at the U.S. Soldiers' and Airmen's Home in Washington, D.C. Before a group of Korean War veterans, Colonel Choong Soon Kang thanked all those who had served in Korea and explained that "all freedom-loving people around the world are eternally grateful to you."[97] It may have taken nearly fifty years, but Korean War veterans and POWs were, at last, beginning to feel appreciated.

✯ Notes ✯

Introduction: Forgotten Soldiers of a Forgotten War

1. Quoted in Harry J. Middleton, *The Compact History of the Korean War*. New York: Hawthorn Books, 1965, p. 210.
2. Quoted in Lewis H. Carlson, *Remembered Prisoners of a Forgotten War*. New York: St. Martin's Press, 2002, p. 250.

Chapter 1: The Long Journey Northward

3. Quoted in Raymond B. Lech, *Broken Soldiers*. Urbana: University of Illinois Press, 2000, p. 17.
4. Quoted in Arthur W. Wilson, ed., *Korean Vignettes: Faces of War*. Portland, OR: Artwork Publications, 1996, p. 209.
5. Quoted in Wilson, *Korean Vignettes*, p. 283.
6. Quoted in Carlson, *Remembered Prisoners of a Forgotten War*, pp. 103–4.
7. Larry Zellers, *In Enemy Hands*. Lexington: University Press of Kentucky, 1991, pp. 90–1.
8. Quoted in Zellers, *In Enemy Hands*, p. 91.
9. Quoted in Carlson, *Remembered Prisoners of a Forgotten War*, p. 76.
10. Quoted in Zellers, *In Enemy Hands*, p. 113.
11. Quoted in Carlson, *Remembered Prisoners of a Forgotten War*, p. 109.
12. Quoted in Harry Spiller, ed., *American POWs in Korea: Sixteen Personal Accounts*. Jefferson, NC: McFarland, 1998, p. 49.
13. Quoted in Spiller, *American POWs in Korea*, p. 87.

Chapter 2: The Permanent Camps

14. Quoted in Spiller, *American POWs in Korea*, p. 50.
15. Quoted in Spiller, *American POWs in Korea*, p. 107.
16. Quoted in Carlson, *Remembered Prisoners of a Forgotten War*, p. 124.
17. Quoted in Carlson, *Remembered Prisoners of a Forgotten War*, p. 124.
18. Quoted in Spiller, *American POWs in Korea*, p. 21.
19. Quoted in Spiller, *American POWs in Korea*, p. 88.
20. Quoted in Carlson, *Remembered Prisoners of a Forgotten War*, p. 154.
21. Quoted in Carlson, *Remembered Prisoners of a Forgotten War*, p. 156.
22. Quoted in Max Hastings, *The Korean War*. New York: Simon & Schuster, 1988, p. 292.
23. Quoted in Carlson, *Remembered Prisoners of a Forgotten War*, p. 160.
24. Quoted in Rudy Tomedi, *No Bugles, No Drums: An Oral History of the*

Korean War. New York: Wiley, 1993, p. 229.

25. Quoted in Henry Berry, *Hey Mac, Where Ya Been?* New York: St. Martin's Press, 1988, p. 199.

26. Quoted in Carlson, *Remembered Prisoners of a Forgotten War,* p. 174.

27. Quoted in Carlson, *Remembered Prisoners of a Forgotten War,* p. 175.

28. Quoted in Carlson, *Remembered Prisoners of a Forgotten War,* p. 28.

Chapter 3: The War Inside the Camps

29. Quoted in Middleton, *The Compact History of the Korean War,* p. 211.

30. Quoted in Brian Catchpole, *The Korean War.* New York: Carroll & Graf, 2000, p. 213.

31. Quoted in Lech, *Broken Soldiers,* p. 92–3.

32. Quoted in William Lindsay White, *The Captives of Korea.* New York: Charles Scribner's Sons, 1957, p. 105.

33. Quoted in Carlson, *Remembered Prisoners of a Forgotten War,* p. 181.

34. Quoted in Eugene Kinkead, *In Every War but One.* New York: Norton, 1959, p. 108.

35. Quoted in Lech, *Broken Soldiers,* p. 96.

36. Quoted in Lech, *Broken Soldiers,* p. 96.

37. Quoted in Spiller, *American POWs in Korea,* p. 54.

38. Quoted in Carlson, *Remembered Prisoners of a Forgotten War,* p. 177.

39. Quoted in Spiller, *American POWs in Korea,* p. 36.

40. Carlson, *Remembered Prisoners of a Forgotten War,* p. 189.

41. Quoted in Lech, *Broken Soldiers,* p. 103.

42. Quoted in Lech, *Broken Soldiers,* p. 121.

43. Quoted in Lech, *Broken Soldiers,* p. 124.

Chapter 4: Keeping Hope Alive

44. Quoted in Lech, *Broken Soldiers,* p. 150.

45. Quoted in Carlson, *Remembered Prisoners of a Forgotten War,* p. 190.

46. Quoted in Carlson, *Remembered Prisoners of a Forgotten War,* p. 90.

47. Quoted in Malcolm McConnell, "Johnson's List," *Reader's Digest,* January 1997, p. 52.

48. Quoted in Carlson, *Remembered Prisoners of a Forgotten War,* p. 91.

49. Hastings, *The Korean War,* p. 301.

50. Quoted in Spiller, *American POWs in Korea,* p. 70.

51. Quoted in Carlson, *Remembered Prisoners of a Forgotten War,* p. 188.

52. Quoted in Hastings, *The Korean War,* p. 301.

53. Quoted in Spiller, *American POWs in Korea,* p. 139.

54. Quoted in Carlson, *Remembered Prisoners of a Forgotten War,* p. 131.

55. Quoted in Carlson, *Remembered Prisoners of a Forgotten War,* p. 155.

56. Quoted in Clay Blair, *The Forgotten War: America in Korea, 1950–1953.* New York: Times Books, 1987, p. 963.

57. Quoted in Carlson, *Remembered Prisoners of a Forgotten War,* p. 216.

58. Quoted in Lech, *Broken Soldiers,* p. 177.

59. Quoted in Virginia Pasley, *22 Stayed.* London: W.H. Allen, 1955, p. 219.

60. Quoted in Carlson, *Remembered Prisoners of a Forgotten War*, p. 182.
61. Quoted in Tomedi, *No Bugles, No Drums*, p. 231.
62. Quoted in Carlson, *Remembered Prisoners of a Forgotten War*, p. 144.
63. James Thompson, *True Colors: 1004 Days as a Prisoner of War*. Port Washington, NY: Ashley Books, 1989, p. 118.

Chapter 5: A Bittersweet Freedom

64. Quoted in *Korean War Stories*, produced by New Voyage Communications, PBS Home Videos, 2001.
65. Quoted in James L. Stokesbury, *A Short History of the Korean War*. New York: Quill, 1990, p. 236.
66. Quoted in Spiller, *American POWs in Korea*, p. 109.
67. Quoted in Thompson, *True Colors*, pp. 121–2.
68. Quoted in Lech, *Broken Soldiers*, p. 184.
69. Quoted in Tomedi, *No Bugles, No Drums*, p. 232.
70. Thompson, *True Colors*, p. 138.
71. Quoted in Berry, *Hey Mac, Where Ya Been?* p. 200.
72. Quoted in Tomedi, *No Bugles, No Drums*, p. 233.
73. Quoted in Carlson, *Remembered Prisoners of a Forgotten War*, p. 215.
74. Quoted in Lech, *Broken Soldiers*, p. 203.
75. Lech, *Broken Soldiers*, p. 204.
76. Quoted in Spiller, *American POWs in Korea*, p. 91.
77. Quoted in Carlson, *Remembered Prisoners of a Forgotten War*, p. 213.
78. Quoted in Spiller, *American POWs in Korea*, p. 110.
79. Quoted in Carlson, *Remembered Prisoners of a Forgotten War*, p. 225.
80. Quoted in Carlson, *Remembered Prisoners of a Forgotten War*, p. 228.

Chapter 6: Legacy of an Unpopular War

81. Quoted in Lech, *Broken Soldiers*, pp. 270–1.
82. Quoted in Carlson, *Remembered Prisoners of a Forgotten War*, p. 189.
83. "Why G.I.'s Folded," *Newsweek*, January 26, 1959, p. 104.
84. *The Manchurian Candidate*, George Axelrod and John Frankenheimer, prods., John Frankenheimer, dir., Metro-Goldwyn-Mayer, 1962.
85. Quoted in Lech, *Broken Soldiers*, p. 208.
86. Quoted in Carlson, *Remembered Prisoners of a Forgotten War*, p. 227.
87. Quoted in Spiller, *American POWs in Korea*, pp. 35–6.
88. Quoted in Carlson, *Remembered Prisoners of a Forgotten War*, p. 239.
89. Quoted in Carlson, *Remembered Prisoners of a Forgotten War*, pp. 242–3.
90. Quoted in McConnell, "Johnson's List," p. 50.
91. Quoted in McConnell, "Johnson's List," p. 52.
92. Quoted in McConnell, "Johnson's List," p. 54.
93. Quoted in McConnell, "Johnson's List," p. 55.
94. Quoted in Spiller, *American POWs in Korea*, p. 162.

95. Quoted in Catherine Walsh, "Perspectives," *America*, vol. 173, no. 5, August 26–September 2, 1995, p. 5.

96. Quoted in Rod Paschall, *Witness to War: Korea*. New York: Berkley Publishing Group, 1995, p. 203.

97. Quoted in Rudi Williams, "38 U.S. Retirement Home Residents Get Korean War Medal," DefenseLINK News, American Forces Information Service News Articles, April 12, 2001.

★ For Further Reading ★

Brent Ashabranner, *Remembering Korea: The Korean War Veterans Memorial.* Brookfield, CT: Twenty-First Century Books, 2001. Tells the story behind the building of this long-overdue memorial to those who fought in Korea. The book has excellent color photos of the memorial and the dedication ceremony as well as black-and-white photos and a brief history of the war itself.

Tom McGowen, *The Korean War.* New York: Franklin Watts, 1992. A well-organized look at the events of the Korean War. Includes descriptions of the personalities of the leaders involved as well as an explanation of why this war had such a major impact on the world.

Don J. Snyder, *A Soldier's Disgrace.* Dublin, NH: Yankee Books, 1987. The story of U.S. Army major Ronald Alley, who was found guilty of collaboration after returning from three years in a North Korean prison camp. Author makes the case that Alley was neither a collaborator nor a traitor but a victim of the era's anti-Communist hysteria.

R. Conrad Stein, *The Korean War: "The Forgotten War."* Hillside, NJ: Enslow Publishers, 1994. A clear and concise overview of the causes and the outcome of the Korean conflict.

★ Works Consulted ★

Books

Henry Berry, *Hey, Mac, Where Ya Been?* New York: St. Martin's Press, 1988. Contains numerous oral accounts of marines who fought in Korea, including the story of a general who successfully resisted indoctrination by his captors.

Albert D. Biderman, *March to Calumny: The Story of American POWs in the Korean War.* New York: MacMillan, 1963. Attempts to correct the widespread misinformation about Korean War POWs and their alleged collaboration with the enemy. The book was conceived as an answer to critics like Kinkead.

Clay Blair, *The Forgotten War: America in Korea, 1950–1953.* New York: Times Books, 1987. A big book that provides insight into how and why the U.S. Army was so poorly prepared for combat when the war first broke out in 1950.

Lewis H. Carlson, *Remembered Prisoners of a Forgotten War.* New York: St. Martin's Press, 2002. A thorough and sympathetic account of the Korean War POW experience. Intersperses historical context with prisoners' first-person recollections.

Brian Catchpole, *The Korean War.* New York: Carroll & Graf, 2000. A history of the war from a British perspective by a former British officer. POW chapters contain accounts that have not appeared in other books.

Jennie Ethell Chancey and William R. Forstechen, *Hot Shots: An Oral History of the Air Force Combat Pilots of the Korean War.* New York: William Morrow. An excellent capsule summary of the origins of the war plus a lengthy account by a pilot who was shot down, imprisoned by the Chinese, and not released until two years after the truce that ended hostilities.

Philip Deane, *I Should Have Died.* New York: Atheneum, 1977. Deane, a journalist captured by the North Koreans when the war began, provides a particularly vivid description of the helplessness of POWs.

Max Hastings, *The Korean War.* New York: Simon & Schuster, 1988. Author interviewed North Korean and Chinese veterans to provide a unique perspective for this one-volume history of the war.

Laurence Jolidon, *Last Seen Alive: The Search for Missing POWs from the Korean War.* Austin, TX: Ink-Slinger,

1995. Author makes a convincing case for those who believe that not all American POWs came home when the Korean War ended.

Eugene Kinkead, *In Every War but One*. New York: Norton, 1959. This influential book is highly critical of the behavior of American POWs during the Korean War. It was expanded from a magazine article published in 1957.

Raymond B. Lech, *Broken Soldiers*. Urbana: University of Illinois Press, 2000. With court-martial transcripts obtained through the Freedom of Information Act, the author documents the brutal treatment and the sophisticated propaganda techniques used on American POWs.

Harry J. Middleton, *The Compact History of the Korean War*. New York: Hawthorn Books, 1965. One historian's view of the war a decade after it ended.

Ward Millar, *Valley of the Shadow*. New York: David McKay, 1955. A book by one of the very few pilots who made it back to the front lines safely after being shot down. Badly wounded, Millar was captured and then made a miraculous escape.

Rod Paschall, *Witness to War: Korea*. New York: Berkley, 1995. A short but perceptive analysis of the war by a retired army colonel, with a good description of the POW issue. Illustrates how, fifty years after the fact, historians view the conflict in a much different context than they did at the height of the Cold War.

Virginia Pasley, *22 Stayed*. London: W.H. Allen, 1955. Author talked to family and friends of those American POWs who refused repatriation after the war. She found that almost all came from broken homes and were poorly educated.

Stephen E. Pease, *Psywar: Psychological Warfare in Korea, 1950–1953*. Harrisbury, PA: Stackpole, 1993. Although this book focuses more on psychological methods practiced by UN forces, it has a section summarizing the ideas behind the techniques of coercion used on American POWs.

Harry Spiller, ed., *American POWs in Korea: Sixteen Personal Accounts*. Jefferson, NC: McFarland, 1998. Recollections of what it was like to be a POW by sixteen men who survived the camps. Includes accounts of the difficulties these men experienced after their return home.

James L. Stokesbury, *A Short History of the Korean War*. New York: Quill, 1990. A good summary of the war, including its relevance to the battle between the West and communism.

William Stueck, *The Korean War: An International History*. New Jersey: Princeton University Press, 1995. The author looks at the war from an international perspective and concludes that it was, in a sense, the opening battle of World War III.

James Thompson, *True Colors: 1004 Days as a Prisoner of War*. Port Washington,

NY: Ashley Books, 1989. This African American POW's recollections of how the men he was imprisoned with resisted indoctrination and how the Communists tried to drive a wedge between them and white soldiers makes for a gripping story.

John Toland, *In Mortal Combat: Korea, 1950–1953*. New York: Morrow, 1991. A very readable account of the war by a prize-winning historian. Toland stresses how important the POW issue was to the resolution of the truce talks.

Rudy Tomedi, *No Bugles, No Drums: An Oral History of the Korean War*. New York: Wiley, 1993. The author, a Vietnam War veteran, interviewed more than thirty veterans of the Korean War, including POWS. Gives readers an idea of what it was like to be there.

William Lindsay White, *The Captives of Korea*. New York: Charles Scribner's Sons, 1957. A comparison of how POWs on both sides were treated during the Korean War.

Arthur W. Wilson, ed., *Korean Vignettes: Faces of War*. Portland, OR: Artwork Publications, 1996. More than two hundred veterans of the war discuss what they remember in short anecdotes of not more than one or two pages.

Larry Zellers, *In Enemy Hands*. Lexington: University Press of Kentucky, 1991. An American teacher when the Korean War broke out, Zellers spent three years as a Korean War POW. His thoughtful account provides valuable insight into the thought processes of prisoners forced to endure brutality and starvation.

Periodicals

Joseph Galloway, "The 'Forgotten War' Is Finally Remembered," *U.S. News & World Report*, August 7, 1995.

Peter Grier, "U.S. Remembers Its 'Forgotten War,'" *Christian Science Monitor*, July 26, 1995.

"History Today," *American History*, September/October 1994.

Insight on the News, vol. 18, no. 19, May 27, 2002.

Malcolm McConnell, "Johnson's List," *Reader's Digest*, January 1997.

"Moral Mandate for All Americans," *Life*, August 29, 1954.

"The Remembered War," *Newsweek*, August 7, 1995.

"The Sorriest Bunch," *Newsweek*, February 8, 1954.

Catherine Walsh, "Perspectives," *America*, vol. 173, no. 5, August 26–September 2, 1995.

"Washed Brains of POWs: Can They Be Rewashed?" *Newsweek*, May 4, 1953.

"What About Reds Among Freed U.S. Prisoners?" *Newsweek*, August 17, 1953.

"Why G.I.'s Folded," *Newsweek*, January 26, 1959.

Films

Korean War Stories. New Voyage Communications. PBS Home Videos, 2001.

The Manchurian Candidate. George Axelrod and John Frankenheimer, prods. John Frankenheimer, dir. Metro-Goldwyn-Mayer, 1962.

Internet Sources

"Data on Veterans of the Korean War," Office of Program and Data Analyses, U.S. Department of Veterans Affairs, June 2000. www.va.gov.

"Johnson's List," Korean War Project, 2003. www.koreanwar.org.

Websites

All POW-MIA Korean. (www.aiipowmia.com. An alphabetical list of all casualties of the Korean War, including POWs and those listed as missing in action.

Korean War Project (www.koreanwar.org). Korean War Veterans Memorial information.

Korean War Veterans, POWs, and MIA. (http://history1900s.about.com). Contains information, databases, and links to other sites relating to POWs.

✯ Index ✯

★ Picture Credits ★

★ About the Author ★

A former editor at *Reminisce* magazine, Michael J. Martin is a freelance writer whose home overlooks the Mississippi River in Lansing, Iowa. He has written more than a half-dozen books for young people, and his articles have appeared in magazines such as *Boy's Life, Timeline,* and *American History.* His most recent books for Lucent Books were biographies of the Wright Brothers and test pilot Chuck Yeager.